TABLE OF CON...

Preface	**2**
Introduction	**5**
1. Addiction as a Disease	10
2. Introduction to Boundaries	23
3. Understanding the Role Boundaries Play in the Healing Process	31
4. The Core Team	41
5. The Support Team and Other Resources	52
6. Core Team Issues: Anger, Frustration, Manipulation	69
7. Building Relationships with Addicts: Trust and Communication	95
8. Recovery and Relapse	110
9. Addiction in Minors	122
10. Special Situations and Issues	137
A. Dual Diagnosis	
B. Addiction and Violence	144
C. Formal Interventions	150
D. Society and Addiction	152
11. Healing Your Own Life	156

PREFACE

This book is the result of the authors' experiences facilitating and participating in a class for families struggling with drug/alcohol use. Bob Brown taught family classes for 12 years. Mardi and Pat Brown participated in his class and shared the knowledge they had obtained as a result of years of dealing with their own family member's addiction.

It became clear to all of us that family members are on the front lines in the "War on drugs," and that they are not trained for this ongoing struggle. They tend to suffer in isolation as they try to deal with the uncertainty and anxiety created by the stress of their loved one's drug use, and their lack of understanding about what they are facing and how to respond to it. They would arrive at class with the hope that someone was going to finally tell them the "answer." They were so focused on the needs of the drug user that often the needs of the rest of the family became secondary.

The class was a training ground for family members who were open to finding new solutions to the problems presented by having an addict in their family. They shared with the group the fear, anger, helplessness and confusion they experienced trying to both help, and protect themselves from the addict. They demonstrated the courage to take the steps necessary to improve their own lives as they worked to figure out how to be more helpful to their loved one. This is not an easy process.

Usually by the time family members arrive at the point where they are willing to participate in a class and talk openly about the issues drug use has created in their family, they are stressed out, isolated and exhausted. Being in this emotionally and often physically depleted state makes it difficult to process new information or implement new strategies in response to the drug use. Hearing what others were facing, and what they had tried to do to improve their situation, gave strength to participants facing similar challenges. The purpose of this book is to help you find the wisdom and support that people experienced in Bob's classes.

There is plenty of information available about addiction in books and on the internet. What we learned from families is that helping them required more than giving out information. Acquiring information is not that difficult. Discovering what the information means to them in their situation, and how to make use of it to improve their own lives, is both more important and more challenging.

What is not important is whether you choose to "diagnose" your loved one as an addict or alcoholic, or whether you insist that your loved one is not an addict or alcoholic. You have seen troubling behavior and you are concerned, or you would not be reading this. A label is not of much value at this point. **What is important is how you respond to your loved one's behavior and whether you are taking care of yourself.**
In this book we use the word addict. This word will represent addiction, alcoholism, substance abuse,

or problem drinking and is not meant to be a diagnosis of your family member.

We also use the word drug. This will be used to represent alcohol, street drugs, marijuana, methamphetamine, etc. and the misuse of prescription medications.

We hope through the use of this book family members struggling with addiction will gain useful information, reduce their isolation, and learn skills that give them the best chance for success in improving the health and wellbeing of their family.

INTRODUCTION

Trying to deal with an addict in the family is like trying to save someone drowning in deep water. A drowning person lashes out, struggles against anyone trying to save them, and without meaning to, pulls the rescuer down with them.

Having an addict in the family compromises the health and wellbeing of everyone. It creates a constant underlying level of tension, with everyone wondering when the next crisis will occur.

By listening to and working with families, we identified the skills that are essential to counter the ongoing stress substance abuse causes. The skills listed below were used by family members to manage the destructive forces that their loved one's drug use brought into their lives. Utilizing these skills enabled them to take back their lives, helped other family members and provided a lifeline to the addict from a safe distance.

The skills are:

- **How to Create and Maintain Boundaries;**

- **How to Work Effectively as a Team;**

- **How to Find and Use Appropriate Support;**

- **How to Manage Loss of Trust;**

- **How to Give Up Control of Outcomes for the Addict;**

- **How to Improve Communication with the Addict and with other Family Members; and**

- **How to Take Care of Yourself.**

It takes commitment to learn to implement these skills consistently, but the effort you make will be rewarded. The skills will help you take charge of your own environment while you are dealing with a situation that will only become more intolerable over time unless a proactive strategy based on accurate information is developed.

We are not promising that the addict in your family will get clean and stay clean. That may or may not happen. We are offering a path that will ease your pain and promote the well-being of every family member, including the addict.

This book is a tool to be used by individuals or groups. It works for those who want a framework to discuss their own experiences, try new behaviors and learn from the experiences of others.

We minimize the re-telling of horror stories about addicts. Anyone drawn to this book will no doubt have many horror stories of their own. The examples we use will provide a context so that you can determine what is most appropriate to reduce the level of chaos in your family.

What we witnessed in the family class and believe is that what you think affects what you do. What you think about addicts in general, and specifically about the addict in your family affects how you interact with the addict in your daily life. The more accurate your ideas about addiction are, the more effective your actions are likely to be. Although love and good intentions are essential, if they are combined with correct basic ideas you are more likely to get good results.

This book begins with information as to what addiction is and what it is not. This will set the stage for the discussion of what families of addicts can do to improve their own lives. In order to help your loved ones, you need to begin by helping yourself.

Learning the skills that are the foundation of this book is a process that involves practice, repetition, and trial and error. We found that each person and family will learn these skills and implement them in a way that fits their unique situation. This is not a cookie cutter process.

Implementation may require that each family member change some of their ideas and some of their ways of acting and reacting. There can be a period of trial and error before you find solutions that work for you, and even if all the family members agree on the basic concepts, they may still have a hard time agreeing on exactly how to implement a plan of action.

Presenting skills for learning is a fascinating process. We tried to provide the reader with the process used in the class. As a result you will find each skill described in several chapters and in different contexts. For example, information on the skill, "Creating and Maintaining Boundaries," starts in Chapter 2 where a thorough treatment of boundaries is provided. This concept is also discussed in subsequent chapters, but in the context of working as part of a team, in your relationship with the addict in your family, and in learning to reclaim your life from the damaging effects of addiction. Chapter 7 also focuses on boundaries, but in the context of how to manage your loss of trust, give up control of the outcomes for the addict and improve communication with the addict. The seven skills are woven throughout this book so you can get a thorough understanding of using these skills in different situations and learning new behaviors.

Our goal for this book is to help family members understand what they need to know, what they need to do, and how to do it in order to make the changes that will improve the quality of their lives and offer the best chance for them over the long term. This book is for families to help themselves over a lifetime, regardless of whether the addicted person in their family ever gets help, gets help and relapses, gets help and relapses many times or gets help and stays clean and sober. In order to be successful in recovery, both the addict and family members must make changes in their lives.

Our emphasis throughout is on you, the family member or friend of the addict, and the importance of learning to focus your attention on what you can learn to control (your environment and how to manage it in the face of addiction), and away from what you can't directly control (the actions and outcomes for the addict).

When addiction enters a family, the whole family embarks on a journey. We are here to talk about that journey and to share our understanding of what that journey could look like. We believe the skills we present are essential for successfully negotiating that path in a healthy way with the best chance for a positive outcome.

CHAPTER 1. ADDICTION AS A DISEASE.

When people talk about addiction and addicts, their ideas tend to fall into two main categories: the flawed character theory and the disease theory.

The Flawed Character Theory. The flawed character theory tends to be the easier of the two to accept; it appeals to common sense and direct observation of behavior. The addict appears to be making totally irrational and damaging decisions with complete disregard for the consequences his actions have for himself and others. He doesn't usually appear to be out of control in doing these things. When he starts drinking again after two weeks of sobriety, it seems he could choose to stay sober if he really cared about himself and others.

People who subscribe to the flawed character theory often find themselves saying things like this to the addict:

- Why do you keep doing this? Can't you see how unhappy you're making everyone?
- How could you do this to your mother? She was up all night worrying about you. Don't you care?
- How long do you think you can keep doing this before you lose your job, drive your family away, or kill yourself?
- Get a grip on yourself. You don't have to keep acting this way.

- Why don't you just stay away from those junkie friends of yours? They're nothing but trouble.

Later on, we'll look in detail at many of the typical behaviors of addicts and the typical responses of their loved ones, but first we want to describe the other theory of addiction: the disease theory. As you'll see, this is the theory we think is more accurate and more useful as a guide to action.

The Disease Theory. The vast majority of professionals in the field of substance abuse, substance dependency, and addiction have adopted the view that these are medical conditions or diseases that directly impact the central nervous system along with all other systems of the body. Addiction alters the brain and the brain chemistry and changes the way addicted people think and perceive the world.

The most definitive description of the behavior that a person with a serious drug use problem exhibits can be found in the American Psychological Association's **Diagnostic and Statistical Manual of Mental Disorders.** This is the main diagnostic tool used by professionals in the mental health field. The manual does not use the word addiction at all. It classifies substance related disorders as either substance abuse or substance dependence. Both abuse and dependence have seriously damaging effects on the lives of drug users and the lives of those closest to them. The Diagnostic and Statistical Manuel of Mental Disorders describes a substance use disorder as follows:

A maladaptive pattern of substance use leading to clinically significant impairment or distress, as manifested by **one** (or more) of the following, occurring within a **12-month** period:

(1) recurrent substance use resulting in a failure to fulfill major role obligations at work, school, or home (e.g., repeated absences or poor work performance related to substance use; substance-related absences, suspensions, or expulsions from school; neglect of children or household)
(2) recurrent substance use in situations in which it is physically hazardous (e.g., driving an automobile or operating a machine when impaired by substance use)
(3) recurrent substance-related legal problems (e.g., arrests for substance-related disorderly conduct)
(4) continued substance use despite having persistent or recurrent social or interpersonal problems caused or exacerbated by the effects of the substance (e.g., arguments with spouse about consequences of intoxication, physical fights).

These behaviors are directly related to changes in the limbic system, a part of the brain that is very basic and controls our survival instincts and our pleasure center. Because of the ways drugs change this part of the brain, addicts believe that their drug of choice is what makes life worth living: not family; not a career; not relationships; not financial stability. It's all about the drug.

Even while they swear they are not addicted, and they can take the drug or leave it, their actions demonstrate that they value their drug of choice above and beyond all other values. One addict who successfully stopped using after a long in-patient treatment program told his mother: "Until I had been off drugs for six months, I couldn't seriously imagine life without them."

What do the DSM criteria cited above look like in reality? Here are some specific behaviors you can expect to see if your loved one is developing serious issues with substance abuse or dependency.

Behavior Specific to Adolescents or Youth

Substance abusing students often have a noticeable decline in academic performance and lose interest in sports, extra-curricular activities and positive peer relationships. Their sleep patterns may be disrupted causing them to have attendance and truancy problems. They may begin having problems with the police and authority in general.

Family members may feel the youth is unwilling to participate in family outings, obey house rules, keep curfews, and do homework and chores. The youth may seem secretive, hostile, argumentative, unpredictable and difficult to approach. They may be hanging out with friends whose influence is negative. If you notice these things going on and feel your relationship with the youth is deteriorating, it's time to get help before things get worse.

Behavior Common in Adults

Adults with substance abuse issues have similar difficulties that play out in their workplace and home life. They begin to lose the ability to meet their obligations to their family, friends, employer and themselves. Family members may find that the addict has unpredictable mood swings varying from life of the party to angry troll. They may have become increasingly unavailable emotionally and physically. You may no longer feel that you can count on them to show up on time, or at all, for family functions: birthdays, school events, even family meals. Unreliability and secretiveness are often the first signs of a serious problem with alcohol and drugs.

Addicts are often dishonest about how and where they are spending money. They may hide how deeply in debt they've become. They may pressure family members for money to support their habit by using some pretext to cover the true source of their financial difficulty. What they want you to give them money for may sound legitimate: to upgrade their computer, get needed dental work done, etc. But what you observe over time is that they don't use the money for these purposes. They don't return it to you. It just disappears.

They often have problems with their employer and may ask family members to lie for them about their absenteeism, abuse of sick leave and tardiness. They may have received warning letters, been passed over repeatedly for promotion, been demoted or threatened with termination because of their inability to perform reliably.

A mark of addiction is an inability to recognize and take responsibility for the problems substance abuse has created. Everything and everyone else becomes the problem. In the addicts' mind their substance of choice is the solution, not the problem. You are the problem, their employer is the problem, the government, etc.

Another area that may show decline is their self-care. They may lose interest in food, or develop strong cravings for junk foods, especially sweets. Their sleep may become erratic. They may show sudden weight loss, develop skin and stomach problems, generally appear less healthy, and exhibit poor personal hygiene. Addiction tends to narrow the world of the addict; it replaces activities that used to be important.

Has your loved one developed patterns of chronic vague illness, malaise, or unexplained pain? Does he complain of fatigue, headaches, insomnia, irritability, depression, diarrhea, constipation, upset stomach, and a host of other health issues that divert attention to ailments seemingly unrelated to substance abuse, when in fact the underlying problem is the over use of alcohol and/or other drugs?

Do you find yourself thinking or saying to your loved one: "You just don't seem to be yourself lately. Is something wrong"? Addiction, even in its early stages, has a transformative effect, with addicts often seeming very different than they were before. Or, more commonly, they may alternate between who they used to be and the addict they are becoming.

A final pattern worthy of note: when confronted with comments about any of the behavioral changes you've observed, the drug or alcohol user will almost always deny that he has changed or that he has a problem. If pressed, he will often let you know that it is you, not him that has a problem. Typical responses of an addict, wherever he may be on the continuum, are denial and projection. "I don't have a problem. Why are you always nagging me"?

At any age, the misuse of prescription drugs can result in similar attitudes and behaviors. Access to prescription drugs is currently easy, especially in states that have allowed a proliferation of "pain clinics" and other medical fronts for "no questions asked" dispensing of addictive drugs. The increase in prescriptions of psycho-active drugs, especially in the United States, where direct advertising to consumers is allowed, is staggering. Many of these drugs, in addition to being addictive, are extremely dangerous, especially when used in combination with alcohol.

Sadly the normal progression of addiction is deterioration, not improvement or even stability. As your loved one's behavior deteriorates, it becomes more and more difficult to miss the connection between his disfunctional behavior and the use of drugs or alcohol.

Some Characteristics of the Disease

1). Addiction is not personal. Contrary to what the addict would like you to believe, his using is not caused by something you did or said. **What you are seeing are predictable symptoms of the way the disease process changes brain chemistry. This is the reality upon which your actions need to be based.**

Addiction isn't just bad decision making, although bad decisions are an important part of the symptom complex of addiction. It is a medical condition the addict can't just decide not to have, any more than a person can decide not to have diabetes or high blood pressure; but like other chronic diseases, addiction can respond to treatment.

Addiction is a condition that neither the addicted person nor the family members have control over. The behaviors that the addicted person displays are results of the disease acting on the brain/central nervous system. The disease process itself happens primarily in the brain at the cellular level. Changes in the brain are brought on by the repeated use of the drug of choice.

2). Addiction is predictable. For example, denial is a perfectly predictable symptom. Addicts will deny they have a problem with drugs or alcohol, while they continue to lie, cheat, manipulate or steal to get and use their drug of choice. When addiction changes the brain chemistry, it fools the brain into reacting as if something very important and meaningful is happening as a result of the drug use. Actually, nothing at all is happening except the brain is processing the addictive substance with predictable consequences.

Family issues, concerns, and behaviors also show a high degree of predictability because they are dealing with the same disease process. Addicts put themselves and their loved ones through tremendous stress. When family members come to understand that they are witnessing a disease process, it doesn't suddenly solve their problems, but it does provide a framework within which solutions and healthier responses to the addicted person can be found. It allows the family to break the pattern of automatic unhealthy responses to predictable behaviors by the addict and to change the family dynamic in a way that fosters healing for the whole family.

3). **Like all chronic diseases, addiction must be managed over the long term**. Although addicts don't have the option of not having an addiction, the good news is that addicts, like diabetics, can learn to accept that they have an incurable disease and can learn to take responsibility for managing it. With appropriate management, some addicts can and do have normal, productive and happy lives.

Similarly, family members don't have a choice about whether to have an addict in their family, but they do have options about how to deal with the disease. **They have those options whether or not the addict makes healthy choices for himself.**

Addicts need information about their condition. If family members aren't clear about the nature of addiction, it will be hard for them to give clear and accurate information to their loved one. Even though the addicted person will often reject this information, the family member should understand that denial is a normal symptom of the disease and should not take the rejection personally.

When we say that addiction is a chronic disease that neither the addict nor the family members have control over, we don't mean that the situation is hopeless. We're not saying you should throw up your hands and give up on either your addicted loved one or on your own ability to live a happy and fulfilling life. However, since addiction affects the whole family, both the addict and the family members can expect life-changing consequences related to long-term management of the disease.

Those consequences don't have to be entirely negative. Many families have found that learning to work together constructively in dealing with the addiction results in closer, more rewarding family relationships. A common problem, faced together, can result in the positive feeling of mutual support and the satisfaction of reaching common goals and workable solutions.

Family Action Based on the Disease Theory. One of the most difficult and most important things to learn about the disease of addiction is this: as a family member, there are some things you can do something about; there are other things that only the addict can do something about. Learning the difference is a critical step in healing, both for the addict and the family. A correct understanding of addiction as a disease will help the family accomplish its two primary goals: to act consistently toward the addict in ways most likely to support long term recovery; and to deal with the issues of addiction in ways that support family health and cohesion.

"The Three Cs" are commonly used to clarify these issues. "The Three Cs" are: you didn't **Cause** it; you can't **Cure** it; and you can't **Control** it. This can initially sound negative or threatening, but realizing the truth of the Three Cs is actually the beginning of family healing.

As with any chronic condition, the addict must take primary responsibility for managing his illness. **Family members cannot manage the addict's condition no matter how badly they want to or how clearly they think they see the problem or the solution.**

Addicts need to learn to manage their addiction, and family members need to learn to manage their responses to the addicted person they care about. Nagging, preaching, threatening, lecturing or pleading is a waste of time. It's actually worse than a waste of time; it promotes negative dynamics in the family that have the effect of prolonging unwanted behavior.

This is just a description of the disease of addiction. Later we'll talk in great detail about what you can do about it, and how you can begin to replace emotional reactions to your loved one's behavior with planned, purposeful and consistent action.

For now, we'll leave this section on addiction as a disease with the following summary:

- When addicts make bad and hurtful choices as a result of their addiction, that should be no surprise. That's what addicted people do.
- Addiction does not respond to logical thought. Addicted people can be very intelligent in every other aspect of their lives but oblivious to the destruction their addiction causes in their own and their family members' lives.
- Addiction is not personal, although it can affect you deeply because it is hard to see someone you love destroying himself.
- Family members and friends get manipulated by the addicted person they care about. This is the normal dance that occurs with the disease of addiction. Family members will continue to be manipulated until they make a decision to stop allowing this to happen and learn new skills to manage their relationships with each other and the addict.
- Addicts can learn to manage their condition and live a healthy and happy life. While your actions and attitudes can make this more or less likely, **you the family member or friend cannot do this for the addict.**
- The primary challenge for family members of an addict is to gain or regain control over their own lives. Families put themselves through incredible grief and anxiety by focusing on the wrong challenge: **struggling to gain control over the addict's life and behavior.**

DISCUSSION AND EXERCISES

The purpose of these exercises is to give you the opportunity to apply what you have just read to your own situation. If you are reading this book in a group, compare your perceptions with each other, discuss the key ideas in the chapter, and see if there are major similarities or differences of opinion about either what you have read or about your own situations. You may find it helpful, as you read and apply this book, to make notes or even to keep a journal.

1. **What specific changes in behavior have you and other family members noticed that make you think your loved one might be an addict or have serious problems with drugs or alcohol?**

2. **Just as denial is a normal part of addiction, it is normal for family members to struggle with the idea that the loved one has an addiction. Has denial that your loved one has a serious problem with drugs or alcohol affected the ability of your family to deal constructively with the addict?**

3. **Can you identify one behavior you have developed with the addict in your life that you see is counter-productive? Is it something you would like to change?**

CHAPTER 2. INTRODUCTION TO BOUNDARIES.

We all understand the idea of boundary lines in terms of the point at which you cross the U.S. border into Canada, or the property line where you put up a fence to keep the neighbors' dog out of your yard. These are <u>physical boundaries</u> put in place to establish ownership and rules governing behavior. You can't take your gun into Canada, and you can't swim in your neighbors' pool without their permission. If you violate these rules associated with ownership, you expect that there will be negative consequences.

All families have boundaries whether consciously created or not.

<u>Implicit boundaries</u> are the ways we respect another person's privacy and possessions without question and out of habit, because this is our family's traditional way of operating, or as the English say, "It's just the done thing."

Some examples of implicit boundaries might be: we only use our own toothbrushes; we don't go into anyone's purse without their permission; we don't leave the doors of our house unlocked at night.

All families have some form of implicit boundaries, and what those boundaries are can vary greatly.

There are also <u>explicit boundaries.</u> These need to be established when situations arise where someone's behavior is causing problems or tension in the family. This is when there is a need to clarify the personal or family value that is being violated and spell out what the boundary is and what the consequences for violating it will be.

The following is an example of a situation where a parent might feel the need to create and communicate an explicit boundary.

You've allowed your son to use your car when he goes out on dates, but when he comes home at night the gas tank is empty. This inconveniences you. You don't have enough gas to get yourself to work in the morning. You feel angry and resent his lack of gratitude for your generosity.

An example of an explicit boundary you could create would be saying to your son, "I need gas in my car in the morning to drive to work. You will have to make sure I have enough gas to get to work and back when you use my car or I won't be able to continue lending my car to you."

The purpose of establishing boundaries is to let people know what your expectations are and what consequences there will be if they are not met. **You usually establish boundaries in order to prevent misunderstandings and to make your expectations clear.**

Sometimes we discount the importance of having firm <u>emotional bounderies</u> because we feel a strong urge to "be there" for our loved one in distress. When we accept late night calls from someone who is intoxicated, listen to a drunk complain how unfairly they are being treated, or tell us what an inadequate parent we have been, we may be thinking that we are being caring, when in fact we are allowing ourselves to be emotionally drained. This can happen when we ignore how stressful it is for us to give up needed sleep, or what a toll it takes on us to listen to negative conversations that leave us feeling depressed and inadequate.

This is an example of how one mother established an emotional boundary. Her adult son would go into detailed descriptions of incidents where he was badly beaten up while on drunken binges. After hearing these accounts for several years the mother realized how much they increased her fear and anxiety, and that listening to him tell these tales wasn't helping him stop putting himself in danger. She woke up to the fact that this pattern of telling horror stories about his drunken experiences was highly manipulative. Her son was impressing upon her how important it was for her to make sure he had a safe haven in her home and to come rescue him from the street when he called late at night drunk and disoriented.

Once she understood this pattern, she was able to disrupt it with a simple emotional boundary. When her son started to tell one of his horror stories, she stopped him and said, "It's not good for me to hear about the bad things that happen to you when you drink. I don't want you to tell me about those things anymore." Over a period of several months he tried bringing this topic up again a few more times. Each time he did this she calmly repeated exactly the same message. It has now been many years since he tried to bring up this disturbing topic with her.

In our culture we use expressions like, **"I'm drawing a line in the sand, and the buck stops**

here." These sayings dramatize the importance our society places on having clear, firm boundaries. They are necessary to protect public health, safety and property; within families they are especially necessary for peace and harmony in the home.

Establishing boundaries is normal behavior in all our relationships, with our spouses, children, and friends. Some typical examples are: "No phone calls during dinner"; or "Ask permission before inviting a guest to sleep over." With most people, such boundaries are understood, accepted and followed. Since, as we previously discussed, addicts tend to be impulsive and self-centered, boundaries have to be made more explicit. This may require more thought about what areas are problematic, what parts of the relationship with the addict you most need to change and what are some possible boundaries that you are willing and able to enforce.

A BOUNDARY IS WHAT YOU WILL OR WILL NOT TOLERATE, AND WHAT YOU ARE WILLING AND ABLE TO ENFORCE. IF THERE IS NO CONSEQUENCE YOU DON'T HAVE A BOUNDARY.

When dealing with an addict the normal rules of relationships tend to break down. **We may allow the addict to disregard our personal boundaries in a misguided attempt to keep the peace.**

We may placate them to avoid giving them an excuse to use their drug of choice. For example: paying their debts, lending them money, providing them a free place to live, and covering for them with the law, their boss, or other family members. By making allowances for them and not having clearly defined boundaries, we become complicit in what can become an increasingly debilitating relationship.

Positive change in this dynamic doesn't come by acting out of anger or resentment, but by establishing and enforcing well thought out boundaries. This does not mean becoming more rigid or punitive toward the addict. It does mean working on developing more clarity, compassion, and consistency in responding to our loved one's addiction. This helps to accomplish three critical goals: taking back control of our own life and sense of well-being; building a new and more constructive relationship with the addict; and creating the conditions that have the best chance of influencing the addict to seek treatment.

It helps to start facing how addiction has impacted you personally. What are some of the effects having an addict in your family has had on your life? Do you feel free? Do you laugh and have fun often? Do you get enough physical exercise? Are you pursuing your own interests and hobbies? Or is the opposite true? Are you experiencing increased suffering and anxiety, disturbed sleep, social isolation, financial and health problems? Has your world gotten smaller? Do you think you will never be truly happy again? Do you neglect your own health? Is your time spent worrying about and trying to create what you see as a positive outcome for the addict? Answering these questions honestly can be very painful and that is why seeking support from others who have walked in your shoes is so important.

If you are a physical and emotional wreck, you are in no condition to be helpful to anyone else, including the addict in your family. Reacting from a state of panic, desperation or anger is almost never successful. As you begin to strengthen control over your own life, you will discover the energy and focus you need to relate to the addict in more helpful ways.

Setting boundaries is about maintaining your own personal well-being while you are dealing with the realities of addiction in your family. You know you are setting effective boundaries when you feel yourself relaxing and feeling more in control of your life.

In order to create healthy boundaries with an addict, family members need a correct understanding of the baffling disease they are facing. Only a realistic understanding of what is going on with the addicted person we love will give us the ability to understand and establish workable boundaries. That's why we've talked at length about the nature of addiction. As you read the following chapters, you may find it useful to refer back to Chapter One.

Understanding and accepting the power addiction holds over the whole family takes time. Dealing with that reality is a process of becoming more aware of our own actions and motives, paying attention to the effects of our behavior on the addict and other family members, and learning new skills. This takes a commitment of time and a willingness to learn new ways of thinking and behaving.

Some families out of desperation have created <u>absolute boundaries</u>; they have removed the addicted member from any contact with the family.

Most families resort to this solution only because they have been unable to find any other way to ensure the survival of the rest of the family.

Confusion about what it means to establish boundaries can prevent families from taking action on this important task. You may think, for example, that it means being harsh or judgmental, or giving up on and abandoning your loved one.

If families are willing to work together to learn new behaviors based on accurate information about addiction, extreme measures can frequently be avoided.

In the following chapter we discuss how to use a team approach in defining and implementing workable boundaries. Rather than being a negative undertaking, working together on this task can be the beginning of a rewarding journey.

Here are some general guidelines that will help you begin to think about boundaries with the addicted person in your life:

- Don't do things for them that they can and should be doing for themselves.

- Don't prevent them from experiencing the natural consequences of their behavior.

- Don't cover up for their mistakes or try to resolve the embarrassing situations they get into.

- Don't rescue them from financial problems.

- Don't try to fix them.

EXERCISES AND ACTIVITIES

1. Write down several examples of boundaries the car owner in the first scenario might create in response to his son returning the car with an empty gas tank.

2. Think of the pros and cons of each boundary and the son's possible response to them.

3. List some of the implicit and explicit boundaries in your household.

4. Ask other family members to make their own lists, and then compare them.

5. List some of the changes you see in your life as a result of living with someone with a substance abuse problem.

CHAPTER 3. UNDERSTANDING THE ROLE BOUNDARIES PLAY IN THE HEALING PROCESS.

How Boundaries Help Clarify Control Issues.

The response of most families when they first realize there is a member of the family with a "drug problem" is to try to control the symptoms of the disease: the disruptive behavior, the association with other addicts or "bad influences," the irresponsible use of money. We try to "talk sense" to them. We plead with them to stop for their own sake and ours. We try to appeal to their better nature: "Look what you are doing to me. I can't sleep nights. I'm a wreck, and I have to get up early to go to work." We find and pour out their alcohol, search their rooms for drugs, threaten to leave or kick them out. We say things like: "If you go out that door, don't bother to come back."

When we are saying and doing these or similar things, we are spending our time and energy trying to control what we can't control. This can leave us feeling frustrated, angry, powerless, and depressed. We realize at some point that we have not only lost control over the addicted family member, but control over our own lives. The Alcoholic Anonymous definition of insanity is "repeating the same behaviors and expecting different results."

Truly accepting that addiction is a brain disease helps us to start to see the futility of emotional outbursts directed at changing the symptoms of the addict's disease. We wouldn't scream at someone who has cancer and exhibits its symptoms. If we stop nagging, pleading, crying, yelling and threatening, it doesn't mean we have given up or have accepted the unacceptable. It means we have recognized the uselessness of that type of reaction to the addict, and see that we are wasting time and energy repeating ineffective behaviors. Often it takes getting to the end of your rope to be ready to look at new ways of thinking about addiction and relating to the addict.

We can't control the addict's behavior. We do have, or can learn to have, control over two things: our own environment, and how we respond to the addicted person.

When we start taking control of our environment by setting and enforcing boundaries, we disrupt the addict's status-quo. **Instead of the family constantly reacting to the addict's behavior, the addicted person has to make the adjustments.**

This is an example of how one wife dealt with her husband, a "problem drinker" stopping for a "few drinks" after work, and coming home late and drunk. She would normally have dinner ready to feed her family at 6 p.m. Then she would watch the clock turn 6:30, 7:30 etc. becoming more anxious and angry trying to keep the children under control and his dinner warm. If she was able to reach him on the phone, she would ask him why he wasn't home, when he was going to get home, etc. She would complain about how badly the kids were behaving and how upset she was. This was a predictable, established pattern in their life.

She told her support group about this problem. They helped her find the following solution. On a morning when her husband was sober she calmly explained to him that she was having problems controlling their children in the evening. She had talked with a school counselor who had worked with her on creating a schedule for them. In order for her to have time to supervise the children's homework before bedtime they would have to finish dinner by 6:30. So in the future, if her husband wasn't able to make it home at dinner time she would refrigerate the leftovers for him.

He of course tested this boundary. Fortunately, she had a support group that gave her a place to vent her resentment of his irresponsible behavior, while encouraging her to remain calm when dealing with him, and just follow through with her plan. As the family settled into this new routine, the husband got to experience how much he missed them and realized that he would have to change if he wanted his place at the table. More importantly, she brought some order and control into her home environment, and her anxiety and anger about the evening meal diminished. The more you set effective boundaries, the less time you spend being angry.

As we begin to take control of our own environment we ask ourselves: Who or what do we allow in our house? What do we spend money on? How do we allow people to treat us? As we work out the answers to these and other similar questions, preferably not alone, we are learning new ways to react to the pressures addiction has introduced into our lives.

Each of the three questions in the last paragraph sounds simple, but creating thoughtful boundaries that you are willing and able to enforce when you answer them is not easy. In Chapter 4 we discuss how to start working with a Core Team that can assist you in identifying issues you can begin working on, support you in the decisions you make, and help you implement your planned response.

Addiction affects everyone in the family and causes family members to make adjustments in how they relate to each other. The longer the family struggles with addiction in isolation, the more ingrained and unhealthy these adjustments become. It becomes harder and harder to break these negative patterns and learn to manage issues in a healthy way.

For many families, the hardest thing is learning to answer honestly the question: "What are my issues, and what are the addict's issues"? We want so badly to be able to solve the addict's problems! We see so clearly what they should do. If only they would follow our advice. If that approach was successful we wouldn't feel that there is a need for this book. **We wish that pleading, threatening and reasoning with an addict was effective, but hard experience shows us that knowledge, compassion, and firm boundaries, consistently communicated, are what garner the best results.**

If you are busy trying to manage the addict's life, how are you going to manage your own? You will not be able to! As more of your energy goes into trying to create outcomes for the addict, and their life becomes more unmanageable, the life you envisioned for yourself will seem to become impossible. This is absolutely predictable. If you don't learn to have a life of your own, you will fail at having a relationship with the addicted person.

This is true whether or not they get help for their addiction and start living a different lifestyle.

Why are Firm Boundaries Necessary with Addicts?

Addicts may lie and steal, destroying trust among family members. They are not dependable; they let us down. They often associate with individuals whom the rest of the family cannot accept and don't want in their lives. Addicts' behavior is disruptive, giving rise to stressful arguments and conflicts. The crises they create consume a disproportionate amount of time, energy and attention. Other family members often feel resentful, neglected and ignored as they minimize their own needs in response to the high drama created by the addict.

The addict often seems oblivious to the suffering of family members. What he wants is to use his drug of choice successfully and to get the family off his back. This is normal thinking and behavior for the addict. But for the family, the situation is abnormal and painful. That's why special attention to boundaries on the part of the non-addicted family members is so important.

You can't have a normal relationship with someone who is actively abusing drugs and/or alcohol. Healthy relationships between adults have to be based on mutual trust. **A lack of trustworthiness is one of the most consistent symptoms of the disease of addiction**. The issue of having a constructive relationship with an addict in the absence of trust is so critical that we devote a whole section of Chapter 7 to this topic.

Giving up Control of Outcomes for the Addict.

Just as the addict's thought processes are distorted by addiction, your own thought processes can also become seriously distorted by the tension and anxiety created by addiction in your family. You may find yourself having frustrating talks with your loved one that go nowhere, or making plans for them that never work, or trying to be their counselor. One of the hallmarks of not accepting or understanding the nature of addiction is a consuming focus on trying to manage the addict's life, and pushing for specific outcomes that you think will solve everything. Instead, this typically winds up in power struggles, resentment, and added chaos in the family. When your relationship with the addict is driven by these unhealthy emotions, the main issues get pushed into the background, and you are left with a never-ending struggle to manage their life at the expense of your own.

The more effort you put into trying to control the details of their life, the more they will fight against you. When you are trying to fix them, rescue them, or manipulate them, anxiety becomes a major force in driving the relationship. As your anxiety level rises, you lose the ability to deal with situations calmly and rationally. The relationship becomes a series of confrontations separated by periods of anxious avoidance. Paradoxically, in order to improve your relationship with the addict it is necessary to loosen your grip on attempting to manage their life.

Addicts do not respond to logical thought. They get help only if they are allowed to experience the consequences of their addiction. It is highly unusual for an addict who is being protected and sheltered while continuing to use drugs to feel the need to seek help. When you try to control the outcome for an addict, you get in the way of a natural process and you become a distraction. Giving up control of the outcome for the addict means gradually reducing your focus on trying to manipulate the addict to act in certain ways. This increases your ability to focus on the quality of your own life and to make rational decisions about how to respond to your addicted family member.

You are not powerless. However, you may feel powerless if you exhaust yourself trying to control what you have no control over: your addicted family member's behavior. In order to make improvements in your relationship with the addict you must focus on what you do have control over. You have control over your environment, who and what you let into your life, who lives in your home, and how you let people treat you. You also have control over how you respond to the addict. Do you react by walking on eggshells? Are you reacting from fear and anxiety?

You can learn to stop reacting from fear and learn to respond with a plan that is based on accurate information and new skills.

It is important to co-ordinate what you are trying to accomplish with significant others. Addicts are so skilled at manipulation they will divide and conquer if you don't present a united front. This in one reason learning to work as a team is a vital survival skill for family members dealing with addiction.

Taking care of yourself and your family is helpful and appropriate. Rescuing an addict from the consequences of their substance abuse is not effective. It will not help you accomplish your goal of restoring sanity to your relationship. When you deprive addicts of the natural consequences of their addiction, you deprive them of an opportunity to recognize the seriousness of their situation and the need to get help. What you can provide them with is information on where help is available for them: detox facilities, rehab centers, AA, half-way houses, etc. You can assure them of whatever level of support you are honestly able to offer them in seeking sobriety.

"Your loved one's addiction is not your issue." What does this mean? It means, yes it affects you, but you can't manage the addiction for them. That is their responsibility. You have other issues to deal with as a result of their addiction. In order for them to recover from their condition, they must take responsibility for their illness and acknowledge they need help. Then they must begin the process of recovery and learn to manage this chronic condition over time. Nobody else can do it for them. The more others assume responsibility for the addicted person's recovery the less likely they will assume responsibility for themselves. This is similar in some ways to what people who are diabetic or suffer from any chronic disease have to face. They all have to seek appropriate medical care and take responsibility for managing their health issues, which often requires lifestyle changes.

We know from our experience that only the addict can solve the addict's problems by finding and following a program of sobriety.

Addiction in your family can also have a corrosive influence on you personally: your life, your personality, your character. The task ahead of you is to deal with your own anxiety, anger, hurt, embarrassment and guilt, to create healthy boundaries and to give accurate information to the addict without judgment. We don't expect anyone to face this large a challenge without support.

Family members and friends can be very helpful to each other in the process of creating and maintaining boundaries, or they can undermine each other and aid the addict in manipulating the family. To learn to work effectively as a team, the family must be willing to implement new ways of thinking and behaving. Learning new skills is never easy and this underscores the need to seek cooperation and support from significant others.

In the next chapter we discuss how families and friends can develop teams to support you in defining and implementing workable boundaries.

EXERCISES AND ACTIVITIES

Before we go on to more specifics about creating teams, this would be a good time to think about the following:

1. Briefly, tell someone your history with the addict in your life, or write out a short account. How long have you been aware of the problem?

2. What has been your approach to dealing with the addicted person? Are you committed to that approach, or are you open to trying other

approaches that may require some personal change? Are you prepared to try different tactics, observing what works and what doesn't in terms of improving your life and your relationship with the addict?

3. What was your reaction to what we discussed about addicts being responsible for their own recovery? Does that statement make you feel hopeless like, "Then there is nothing I can do?" Or, do you feel empowered knowing you are free to focus on trying to create a better life for yourself?

4. Do you think it is OK for you to be happy and have your own life get better whether or not the addict is willing to get help?

Writing down your responses to some of these questions will be helpful as you continue working on creating effective boundaries.

CHAPTER 4. THE CORE TEAM.

The family members and close friends who make up the Core Team can be very helpful to each other and can have a positive impact on the addicted person. The Team assembles itself because its members are not satisfied with the status quo. They want to change something about their current reality.

If there is an addict in your family who is negatively impacting your life, your natural impulse will be to believe they need to change: they need to get sober; they need to get a job; they need to be more responsible. You have probably told them what they need to do many times. They may argue with you or act like they agree, but either way the problems persist. If you want sustainable change, you must shift your focus away from creating outcomes for the addict and focus on things that are under your control: your own environment, and your response to the addict.

Previous chapters were about the nature of addiction and the importance of creating and maintaining boundaries. This chapter is specifically about how we use that knowledge about addiction and boundaries to create a team that will support making real change in how you and your family members are impacted by addiction.

Creating a team is so important because even small changes in behavior are difficult to maintain without reinforcement and support.

Family Roles.

It is helpful to have some understanding of typical family response patterns. Response patterns are complicated. Often one family member will have more than one pattern, or can switch back and forth between two or more different and even contradictory patterns. But it's important to know that these typical patterns exist. They are just sets of learned behaviors, so it's quite possible to modify them once you recognize they don't produce satisfactory results. Understanding the tendencies of family members helps identify issues and maintain boundaries.

Are you the tough family member? Is your general approach based on anger at the addict, disgust with the addictive behavior, and unwillingness to put up with it anymore? This is the "I'm mad as hell and I'm not going to take it anymore" stance; but then you do keep "taking it," building more anger and resentment toward both the addict and the family members who make excuses for him. Do you see your teammates as soft or irresolute, unwilling to take the actions that are obviously needed? Do you consider your approach to be the correct one, and do you discount the suggestions of other team members as misguided, too soft, or ineffective?

Or are you the softy, the designated enabler, the one who can't stand the thought of the addict having a bad day? Do you find yourself trying to protect the addict from the angry reactions of the tough team member? Do you remind other team members on a regular basis that the addict had a tough childhood, or has always been sensitive, or has emotional or mental issues that affect the addictive behavior? Do you keep trying to trust the addict and make allowances for his behavior because the addict confides about his misery to you and says he is trying to do better? Do you do things for the addict that he could do for himself, hoping that your love and kindness will eventually result in a change in the addict's behavior? Do you suffer the consequences of the addict's behavior rather than allowing him or her to fully face them? Do you take on his problems as your own?

Or maybe you are the optimist in the family. Do you like to point out that things could be a lot worse, that at least the addict in your family isn't violent (or on crack; or suicidal; or pregnant; or in jail)? Do you point out the good qualities of the addict, and the positive steps the addict has taken to get help or stop using? Is it your inclination to be hopeful and to promote the expectation that the problem will resolve itself in time without any big changes by anyone on the team?

Are you the stoic, keeping your emotions inside? Do you maintain the appearance of being emotionally aloof and unaffected by the chaos around you?

Although there are other response patterns, these are the most common.

It's important to realize that these patterns are just emotional styles. There is no "correct" one, or even a preferable one. Although we display our feelings differently, family members all have strong feelings, and generally all want positive outcomes for the addict, themselves, and the other team members.

The tendency of people is to believe their way of seeing things is the correct way, and their way of dealing with a problem is the best or only way. This tendency can be one of the greatest obstacles the Core Team will have to work on.

Conversely, people's ability to listen to each other, to respect others' viewpoints, and to compromise are critical skills each Core Team member can develop to overcome that obstacle.

Personal change is difficult, but the willingness and ability of team members to make at least small changes in their patterns of behavior is absolutely necessary for positive change to occur.

Team Dynamics.

Your Core Team was created for a specific purpose: to help each of you learn how to live healthy and happy lives in spite of having an addict in the family. The level of anxiety and grief you are now experiencing may make this seem impossible. You may feel you will never truly be happy again. But once you've all agreed to set aside time to work on a regular basis toward creating a better quality of life for yourselves, you will begin to counter the natural tendency of addiction to pull families apart.

Once you've identified what your team wishes to accomplish, there are two aspects of successful operation: "task focus" and "team focus." Task focus means that we have to pay attention to how the objectives of the team are progressing. Team focus means we have to pay attention to how the team members are doing, how they interact, how satisfied they are with the team's progress, and how the changes they are implementing affect their relationships.

When discussing what may appear to be a simple goal, it's important to create a safe environment for every team member to feel they can be honest about how they relate to that goal. If a member feels that happiness in the face of addiction is not a possibility, that point of view needs to be treated with respect. Help each member identify a goal that they can set for themselves, something that removes a burden from their shoulders or lightens their load in some way. And then find ways to support each other in easing the stress in the family. It can be as simple as going for a walk together in the evening or identifying the constellations of stars in the night sky. Try doing something different that brings you moments of peace of mind.

Our recommendations for how to proceed with your task of establishing and maintaining healthy boundaries are pretty simple and straightforward. Remember that we are just presenting this approach in order to give you a starting point. We don't think there is one right way to deal with addiction in the family, or one method that's right for all. Each family and each Core Team has to work out its own preferred method.

Following these six steps will assist you in the process of creating and maintaining boundaries.

1. Have each team member identify three to five specific problems in their current relationship with the addict. For example: the addict doesn't listen to you; he comes home in the middle of the night drunk or high and disturbs your sleep; he calls you in the middle of the night and wants you to talk to him at length or do something for him; he is physically threatening or verbally abusive toward you; he is a financial drain and doesn't carry his own weight, etc. Each problem might indicate an area in which boundaries are being violated or ignored, or an area in which no clear boundary has been established.

2. Combine the lists of problems, paying attention to duplication or overlap. As a team, prioritize the list.

3. Choose one specific behavior that all or most of the team members agree is a problem. Try not to pick the most complicated or most difficult problem to begin addressing. Part of what you want to do with this first problem or issue is to use it for team practice. Remember you are just warming up, so pick something of moderate size. For example, don't pick as your first problem getting the addict into a treatment program. That's too big a problem to start with, and it focuses too much on the behavior of the addict. Some that might be more manageable are: the addict calls home at all hours of the night

and disturbs your sleep; or the addict eats your food, but he doesn't perform any household chores.

4. After you agree on one specific problem, break it down into smaller pieces. If the problem is that the addict doesn't help out around the house and creates more work for everybody else, figure out what the "more work" consists of. Is somebody cooking for the addict? Doing his laundry? Doing his dishes? Cleaning up his bedroom? What are the "hassles" the addict is creating? After you break down the "problem" into smaller pieces, you might want to limit your immediate issue to one or two specific behaviors you want to tackle.

5. As you break down the undesirable addictive behavior into smaller pieces, identify behaviors by Core Team members that might contribute to the problem. Is a team member doing things for the addict the addict could or should be able to do for himself? If the addict is leaving his dirty clothes in the laundry room or on the floor of his bedroom, and somebody is doing the laundry and leaving the clean clothes in his room, might that be considered supporting the addict's bad behavior? Does that level of service make it easier for the addict to continue his patterns? What might happen if the Team member stopped being so care-taking? It is important to avoid an accusatory or blaming attitude to

the family member who thinks he is behaving lovingly toward a sick person. It helps to adopt the attitude that we are all doing the best we can as opposed to accusing someone of being an enabler.

6. Pick one thing that team members agree can be changed, and begin to change it. Make sure no team member feels coerced into agreeing with this particular new boundary and that everyone is truly willing to support enforcing it. Decide whether the change is something you need to communicate to the addict, or whether you can just make the change without bringing it up. Maybe the addict won't even notice the change. Maybe after a week or two he'll plaintively mention that he has no clean clothes. You might have discussed as a Team what the appropriate response should be. Don't create big expectations based on a small change, but don't be surprised if even a small change has unexpected consequences. At a minimum, you may have eliminated one piece of extra work or one small hassle associated with the addict. And probably you will have learned something as a Team that you can use in deciding on the next change you want to implement.

Once your team has been able to apply these steps to one problem, and have been able to agree on one change in the behavior of team members, congratulations! You have created a boundary. And you have gained skills in making creative changes to take control of your own lives. Now you can decide what the next problem is that you want to address.

Small changes in the behavior of key team members can have a surprisingly large impact on the relationship between the addict and the team. Generally we recommend against implementing more than one change at a time. Remember that every change is an experiment. Don't give up if something doesn't work the way you envisioned it; talk about it and try to figure out why things didn't work out well. Try to fix whatever went wrong. Don't lose faith or focus.

Alcoholism, drug abuse and other addictions have been referred to as "cunning and baffling diseases." Addicts are capable of truly impressive psychological manipulations based on a thorough understanding of what pushes each team member's emotional buttons. One of the functions of the team is to thwart the addict's attempts to divide the team or to undermine the resolve of whoever the addict perceives as the weak link on the team. We'll talk in some detail in Chapter 6 about the common issues a Core Team can expect to run into as it changes the family dynamic.

How to Communicate a Boundary to an Addict.

When you create a boundary and want to communicate it to the addict, just communicate the decision your team has made. Don't get involved in a discussion about its merits. "I'm not going to take care of your laundry anymore. That's something you can do for yourself." "I'm not willing to lend you my car anymore. You'll need to make other arrangements for your transportation." "It's not OK to come home after 11:00 pm anymore. If you're not home by 11:00 pm, you'll need to find another place to spend the night."

If the addict protests or argues, don't engage with them. Just respond: "It's not working for us the way things are going. This is what we've decided."

If you are inclined to confront the addicted person because you have had enough and are angry and resentful, step back! This is not a helpful attitude or approach for the addicted person or the family. You need to be calm in every conversation you initiate.

When you talk with an addict, be clear that you cannot talk an addicted person out of his medical condition, or threaten him out of it, or beg him out of it, or bribe him out of it, or shame him out of it.

When you do have conversations about your loved one's addiction, make clear, simple statements about yourself, not about the addict. "I am concerned about your addiction and I want you to get help." "I love you very much and your addiction frightens me." "Your father and I support your recovery, but we won't support your addiction."

EXERCISE AND DISCUSSIONS

Exercise. In this chapter we provided you with a process to identify problems and behaviors associated with addiction in the family. We gave only a few examples of problems a family might experience with an addict. Follow this process and begin to develop your own list of behaviors of the addict that you find unacceptable. Be specific; making a list can be very useful. Some issues will loom large for one family member and not be much of a problem for another. Respectful listening will help you identify an issue where you can work together to create a firm boundary.

Discussion 1. As you had your first meetings of the Core Team, what was the experience like for each member? Was it easier than you expected? Was it more difficult? What obstacles if any did you encounter? Were you able to work around them successfully?

Discussion 2. Review the work of the Core Team so far. Consider the two dangers we warned against: the tendency to focus on changes the addict needs to make, and the tendency to focus on changes other Team members need to make. How are you doing with those two dangers?

CHAPTER 5. THE SUPPORT TEAM AND OTHER RESOURCES.

It is important for the Core Team to have resources outside of the family. As your team members learn to work together, you will find that having outside resources helps to reduce your isolation, and gives you a ready source of objective feedback and consultation. We all need mentors, and having them provides the best chance of success.

As you begin to look for support for your Core Team in your community, it's helpful to be as clear as possible about what you need in terms of support and also what to look out for or avoid.

Here are some of the kinds of support your Core Team may need:

- Expertise about addiction and the way it affects families;

- A safe place for family members to vent their feelings and frustrations and to get the emotional support needed for personal change;

- A place to go and people to talk with who can bring objectivity and experience to issues that tend to bring out intense emotions and push personal buttons;

- A sounding board for specific ideas the Core Team is considering, or to help understand why a particular idea isn't working the way the Team thought it would.

- Help for team members to understand and resolve differences or disagreements that are hindering their effectiveness.

You will note that there are different types of support that might be helpful. Sometimes it is not possible to find all the elements of support your team needs in one place.

Since people's circumstances vary so much, we can only give general guidance for finding a Support Group or other sources of assistance for your Core Team. Do you live in a large city or in a rural community? What kinds of community services are available? Is your church or synagogue or community center active in social issues like addiction, or is help from those sources unlikely?

Here are some possibilities:

- Check the internet; Google "addiction treatment," "alcohol treatment," "Help for families living with addiction," or similar titles along with your location. You may be able to identify helpful resources such as addiction treatment facilities, addiction and/or alcoholism advice hot lines, etc. Many treatment programs include training or education for family members of addicts, and some of them don't require that you actually have a family member in their program in order to attend.

- Look in the Yellow Pages under a variety of related topics such as "addiction," "alcohol abuse," "addiction information and referral," "Alcohol Abuse & Addiction Information and Referral," or "alcohol and drug abuse hotline."

The following is a list of resources that will assist you in using the information in this book:

- For information on getting help for parents with an addicted child of any age and families of teens, refer to the following websites.
  www.ncadd.org
  www.becauseiloveyou.org
  www.parentpathway.com

- For information on how family members can work together to develop an environment that is conducive to the health of the entire family, including the drug user.

  www.familiesandaddiction.blogspot.com
  www.thecounselingcenter.org/The_Counseling_Center/10Ways.html
  www.spiritualriver.com/how-can-i-help-an-alcoholic-or-drug-addict-specific-things-you-can-do-to-help/

- The following organizations can be helpful when reaching out to others in order to

reduce isolation and get information or support.
>   **www.alanon.org**
>   **www.familiesanonymous.org**
>   **www.aa.org**
>   **www.na-hawaii.org**
>   **www.crystalmeth.org**
>   **www.clergyrecovery.com**
>   **www.sobermusicians.com**
>   **www.jbfcs.org/jacs**
>   **www.smartrecovery.org**

The resources that we have recommended are organizations that understand addiction and the issues that family members are struggling with.

Some places one might seek advice or feedback could be hurtful or toxic. Here are some danger signs to look for in assessing the value of a resource:

- Does a resource give us the message that we are responsible for our loved one's addiction, label us, or imply that we "should do something" to fix the addict's problem?

- Does the resource propose simple or single solutions to the Core Team's issues?

- Does engaging with the resource leave us feeling helpless, guilty, or defeated?

- Does the resource focus solely or primarily on the addict's issues rather than the issues of family or Core Team members?

Here are a few examples of simple or single solutions to be wary of:

- You should do a formal intervention to get the addicted person into treatment.
- You can't do anything until the addict wants help.
- There's no way to make things better as long as the addict is living at home. You need to kick him or her out.
- The addict in your family hasn't hit bottom yet. Until he does, there's little you can do.
- You need to adopt a particular religious point of view in order to be helped.
- Your problem is that you are enablers.

There is a grain of truth in almost all of these bits of advice. The problem is that many of these statements are entirely about the addict and just lead you into more of the same theme of allowing the addict or addiction to control your life. There are things you must do whether or not the addict ever gets help if you want to improve the quality of your life.

Using resources is part of a process that should help you in understanding what you are dealing with when you have an addicted person in your family. Positive and effective resources help you reduce your feelings of isolation and anxiety. They help you in relating to your entire family, including the addicted person, in more constructive ways. Good support helps you to understand your own emotions and thoughts and to feel better about yourself. **Most importantly, a good Support Team**

will help your Core Team work toward its own answers and solutions. Beware of quick and facile solutions handed down with authority.

After the Core Team has been formed, weekly meetings with a Support Team are usually very important, if not essential. You may need a month of meetings before you even take the first step to implement any changes in your lives or your behavior toward the addict. Eventually, once the Core Team is functioning smoothly, you may just need to check in with your Support Team periodically.

It's OK to try out various types of support. Just as everything you do initially in your Core Team should be looked at as an experiment, so should your attempts to find support. If the support gives you the things you need to make progress as a Core Team, it's good support. If it doesn't, look elsewhere.

Using your Support Team and Other External Resources to Improve Your Relationship with the Addicted Family Member

In the first section of this chapter we have focused on the general issue of resources for your Core Team. The following section elaborates on how to use those resources to help you and your Core Team members resolve issues or problems as you begin to work at reclaiming your family's life that has been "taken hostage" by the addict.

Having a relationship with the addict requires more thought and more effort than relationships with friends or other family members. This is because addicts are generally less able to be sensitive to or responsive to the needs of others. Responsibility for shaping the relationship in a satisfactory way is part of the new set of skills that you can learn. Is it worth the effort? Only you can answer that question for yourself. We suggest that, if you choose not to totally exclude the addict from your life, it's better in the long run to work on improving your part of the relationship than it is to put up with the status quo.

One thing that all friends and relatives of addicts become familiar with is the repetitive nature of the crises and other typical situations that go along with addiction. We've all had that sinking feeling: "Oh no, here we go again."

You can turn that depressing repetitiveness to your advantage. Each repetitive pattern you can identify and understand provides an opportunity for you to plan a response that will be more effective than what you've said and done in the past. Your Support Team, if it is an effective resource, can help you make sure your planned response meets the essential requirements for an effective interaction with an addict. Before we go into some examples, let's lay out those requirements.

- Your response to the addict must be honest and accurate. Addicts learn to be masters of BS, and they can probably detect yours even better than you can detect theirs. Often we avoid honesty out of fear of the possible response. As you will see, we think that honesty, along with the other requirements, to some extent disarms the addict.

- Your reaction to the repetitive situation you're trying to address must be respectful of the addict. A common response to this second requirement is that if the response is honest, it won't be respectful. This is a serious concern, which the examples will clarify. Addicts don't need heavy judgments dumped on them. They do that for themselves. Typically they already have low self-esteem and see themselves as worthless bums, hopeless, a burden on their families, etc. You won't improve your relationship by joining this chorus of accusation and attack, however justified it may seem.

- Your response must be well thought out, and delivered calmly and without negative judgment. If it is, you'll find that your response won't involve talking about the addict very much, but talking about your own feelings and needs. You need to make these explicit, because you can't expect the typically self absorbed addict to be sensitive to your feelings or needs.

- Your response must be one that can be easily summarized for repeated use, since it is designed to deal with repetitive situations. Your message should be one that you can easily refer back to when the same situation arises again. You want to be able to deliver the same message in shorthand: "Remember the last time this came up and I told you XXX."

The following scenarios provide examples of the kinds of relationship issues family members typically bring to a Support Group, along with the advice they might receive from the group. Part of what we would like to accomplish with these scenarios is to give you a model of how a Support Group can help you with your relationship issues. These "made up" scenarios are actually edited versions of many similar conversations that took place in our Family Group.

Scenario 1.

A couple comes to the group for the first time. When they are asked to talk about their issues, the husband starts:

"Our adult son has been addicted to cocaine for twelve years. During that time he has not held a job or completed a college course. He seldom goes more than a month or two without a relapse. But every week or so he will initiate a long, detailed discussion about some plan he has come up with, plans usually involving major educational programs or professional business careers. I don't want to just shoot him down, but it's driving me crazy trying to act like this is a serious discussion with some relationship to reality."

The leader may ask: "When your son brings this up, what would you really like to tell him?"

The parent responds: "I want to say, 'Why are you talking about getting a Master's degree or getting a government job when you can't even keep your own room clean? How about a plan to get yourself off drugs for the first time in twelve years before you start career planning?"

Group Leader: "I think whatever response you make should be honest, like what you just said. But it should also be respectful of your addicted son. Also, it should be something you could use every time this situation arises. Do you think that would be possible?"

Parent: "I doubt it. When my son launches into his "long range planning" conversation, I don't feel very respectful. If I'm honest, what will come through will be my disgust at how he's wasting his life and still manages to carry on this self-deception."

Group Leader: **"If your response can't be both honest and respectful, then no response at all is better.** Why do you think your son keeps bringing this subject up?"

The wife answers, after a pause: "I think it's his way of asking us not to lose hope in him. He wants us to think that in spite of everything he still has some potential to accomplish something."

Group Member: "Is that something you feel any respect for: his desire for you not to lose hope?"

Wife: "Yes. It's touching that he still doesn't want us to give up on him."

61

Husband: "I do have some respect for his keeping some hope for the future after all he's been through. I just wish it could be more realistic."

Group Leader: "So there is some basis for real respect in what you could respond to him. Let me try out something I can imagine you saying to your son, and then you can tell me what sounds real and what doesn't. Imagine that he has just started in on this conversation that you're so familiar with, and you break in:

'You know, I've been thinking about how you make plans for the future. That always brings up a lot of feelings in me. I think it's because I've always had high hopes for you, and I've always thought that if you could find a way to stop using drugs, you could still accomplish a lot in your life. But I know that as long as you can't stay clean for more than a few months at a time, any long range plans aren't very realistic.

"When you start talking about school or a job, that's what I always think to myself: If only you could get off drugs, these things would be possible. As long as you're using, these plans are just wishes with no reality to them.

"So I've decided I'm not going to get involved in any more conversations with you that involve long range plans that require you to be drug-free. Instead, I want to just remind you that I never lose hope. I've always thought you could find a way to get off drugs if that was the one most important thing you were trying to do. And if you could stay off drugs, anything might be possible.

"Once you manage to go drug-free for six months, I'll remind you of this conversation and we'll talk about plans all you want to. Until then, let's find something else to talk about.

"Like, how about if you and I fix dinner together."

Discussions like this in a support group can help family members who have given up on their ability to have an honest conversation with the addict in their family. The parents can write out their version of a similar statement they would like to be able to say to their child. They can even practice it in the group if they find that helpful.

If they manage to say some but not all of this to their son, they can come back to the group and discuss how it went.

And they can develop a shorthand version to use if their son continues to want to talk long range plans without adequate sobriety. You could say, for example: "Remember what I said about long range planning. I don't want to talk about plans without the six months of sobriety. That's something I know you can do, and it has to come first."

Hopefully, as you read this scenario, you are reminded of the discussion about boundaries in the last three chapters. What the Support Group has just done is to help you move toward defining and communicating a boundary to the addict in your family. **Notice how the process starts by identifying a specific issue that's causing you special irritation or grief, and moves toward**

creating a boundary to protect you without attacking the addict. The Core Group could discuss this boundary at its next meeting and decide whether all members want to adopt the boundary and respond similarly to the addict when the particular situation arises.

Scenario 2.

Two sisters, 23 and 21, come to their first meeting of a Family Group at an Addiction Treatment Center. The older sister, Beth, is married; the younger, Malia, works full time and lives in an apartment with another young woman. They have come to the meeting because of their concerns about their family: their father is drinking excessively and has recently lost his position in a law firm; their mother is distraught at the deterioration in her husband and worried about their financial situation; and their younger brother, 17, is starting to show signs of problems at school and is becoming more difficult for his parents to manage.

The sisters have told their mother about the Family Group and encouraged her to come with them, but she is concerned about her husband's possible reaction.

Group member: "Would you say you've come to this group mainly because of the impact this situation has on your own lives, or is your main concern for your mother, or your mother and brother?"

Malia: "Mainly for our mother and brother, but it's

been getting harder and harder for Beth and me to have any kind of decent relationship with the rest of the family too. There's always some kind of crisis going on, and every time we go home to visit, Dad's drinking is all we talk about. He's usually not even there."

Group Member: "What is your mother afraid might happen if she comes to the group?"

Beth: "She hardly goes anywhere in the evenings any more. I think she feels like she has to be home for our brother, and she never knows when she'll need to handle some situation with our Dad. Plus, I think she's afraid Dad would be really angry if he knew she was coming to a group like this. He would think she was working against him."

Group Member: "In this kind of situation, you all really need to work together and support each other. That's not working against the alcoholic. Having an alcoholic in the family puts incredible strain on the whole family, as you're experiencing. The family members not only need each other more than ever; they also need some support from a group like this to help figure out how to deal with the situation. I'd like to make a couple of suggestions for you to think about:

"One, it's going to be hard for your mother to handle this without help. It would be good for her if she could come with you to a couple of meetings to at least see for herself whether we can be helpful to her.

"Two, this could be really important for your brother. By the way, he's not too young to come with your mother to the meetings. It might be useful for him to see that his situation isn't unusual or disgraceful, however difficult it is.

"Three, the four of you might need to be a little more organized about dealing with this than you are now. I'm talking about maybe planning to get together once a week or so to talk about how things are going and what you all, as a family, might do that would be helpful.

"Four, I can tell you that situations like this don't tend to get better by themselves. If you think of alcoholism as a disease, the prognosis without successful treatment is gradual deterioration. Even if you can manage things the way they are now, you should be thinking about what comes next.

"Finally, I know it can be scary imagining your father's reaction to his wife coming to a meeting to talk about "his problem." But he also probably realizes on some level that he's in big trouble, and sometimes having the family go outside for help can be a real wake-up call for an early-stage addict. At some point your mother is going to have to do something about this, and it would probably be easier and more effective now than later. If he confronts her about it, she should be prepared to explain as calmly and clearly as she can that (1) their current situation has put her under a lot of pressure and anxiety; (2) she needs help dealing with it, and she doesn't feel that he's in any condition to provide the help; (3) she believes that he has a serious problem with drinking and that he needs to seek help himself to deal with that problem. She could mention that the place she is going also has meetings for people with drinking problems, and suggest he start going."

Malia: "That sounds really depressing. But I guess the reason we came here is that we could see for ourselves that things have been getting worse and worse. Beth, do you think we could talk her into coming next week?"

Beth: "At least I think we should try. She might be more likely to do it if she knows our brother can come, and that it might be helpful for him."

Group Member: "You're welcome to come any time, with or without your mother and brother. We're all very familiar with what it's like to have a drug or alcohol addict in the family, and we'd like to help any way we can."

We could go on for another hundred pages following this scenario, with the mother and brother coming to a meeting, and six months of meetings to come, as the family story unfolds. But each family, however similar the stories begin to sound, is unique in its approach and in the solutions that emerge as they work together and work with external sources of support.

The critical things are for family members to work together to deal with the scourge of addiction, and for the family to find adequate sources of support and assistance.

Activities

1. Have each team member identify and visit one community resource and report back to the team about it.

2. Choose one or more of the resources to attend together.

CHAPTER 6. CORE TEAM ISSUES: ANGER, FRUSTRATION, MANIPULATION.

In Chapter 4 we noted some of the obstacles commonly encountered by members of the Core Team:

- The tendency to focus on the addict and the changes we believe the addict should make;

- The tendency for team members to focus on the changes they think other team members should make;

- The tendency for Core Team members to engage in endless discussion of the problems related to the addict's behavior without coming to a consensus about what actions to take.

In this chapter we want to discuss certain issues that are most likely to come up while working together in a group. These issues include:

- Anger and resentment directed toward the addict and other team members;

- Frustration with team dynamics and team progress;

- Backsliding or relapsing to old behaviors by team members;

- Using manipulation rather than straightforward communication;

- Holding onto old family roles and emotional styles in spite of the need for change.

For all of these obstacles and issues there are skills that can be developed and used to counter problems as they arise. For example, active listening and other communication skills can help offset the tendency to think only other team members need to change. Specific skills related to working in groups can help the team avoid unproductive and frustrating meetings where nothing gets resolved.

How to Manage Anger and Resentment toward the Addict

As the Core Team begins to meet, it will become clear that some team members have strong unresolved negative feelings toward the addict: anger, anxiety, hurt, disappointment, guilt. All of these feelings are completely understandable. However, acting toward the addict out of these feelings is not likely to give you good results.

It's not that these feelings are "bad" or "unacceptable"; it's simply that acting out of them is not effective and will not help you accomplish your goals of creating and maintaining a healthy life for yourself and being of assistance to your loved one. That doesn't mean you don't need to deal with these natural and inevitable feelings. We'll talk in Chapters 7 and 8 about healthy ways to do this.

There are two effective antidotes to anger against the addict.

The first is real acceptance of the idea that addiction is a disease. The more you can internalize and emotionally accept this concept, the more you will be able to understand that the addict's actions are not personal, and that your personal angry response is not helpful. Don't expect to "get" this idea in a sudden flash of insight. Understanding addiction as a disease is a process that takes time, willingness, and keen observation.

The second antidote is simply to observe as often as necessary how ineffective angry responses are in solving any of the problems related to addiction. You can learn to understand **in practice, not just intellectually,** that if you are constantly angry with the addict you have an issue that you need to deal with. You can learn that looking to the addict for a solution to the problem of **your** anger is as futile as the self-destructive behavior you see the addict repeatedly using to "solve" **his** problems.

As you begin to internalize the truth that anger at the addict is unproductive and actually unhealthy for you, you can explore the possibility of alternate ways of responding to the addict's behavior. This exploration fits into the process of working with your Core Team to set and maintain boundaries. If you are regularly angry with the addict for not returning your car when he agreed to, and returning it with an empty gas tank, you are ready to create a boundary that limits or eliminates the addict's use of your vehicle. If you are furious every time the addicted family member calls you for help in the early hours of the morning, it's time to work on boundaries related to that behavior.

Anger toward the addict is almost always a symptom of non-existent or ineffective boundaries. The more effective your boundaries become, the more your anger at the addict will decrease. **One of the primary goals of the Core Team is to substitute effective boundaries for emotionally negative ways of dealing with addictive behavior**.

How to Manage Anger toward Other Core Team Members

Addiction has a corrosive effect on family relationships. By the time you get around to forming a Core Team, your own relationships with other family members may have already been seriously damaged. Parents of an addicted family member may have spent years resenting each other, as well as their addicted offspring. It is common among parents of adult addicts for one parent to see the other as mean, cold, and unfeeling; or to see the other parent as soft and weak, a sabotaging coddler who cares more about the addicted individual than about the spouse. This type of anger and resentment comes to the team with its members, and must be dealt with at some point if the team is to make progress. Help from external resources is often necessary.

Sometimes siblings of an addict will take sides with one parent against the other. Siblings may be angry and resentful at the way the brother or sister who is addicted gets special treatment. Very commonly these feelings are not verbalized.

When the tasks of a team are slowed down or stopped by interpersonal resentments, it is important to stop working on tasks and deal with the emotions before moving on. It is all part of the learning and healing process.

Here is an example where resentments as well as fear and guilt get in the way of the team. In a previous chapter, we described a situation where Mom and Dad were supporting an addicted adult daughter, giving her a free place to live and providing other financial and personal help. Let's complicate the situation by adding a sibling, a younger son, age twenty-one, who lives with the parents but pays rent and sees how his sister is creating grief and chaos in their lives. He's angry that his sister can't see how damaging her addiction is, and he advocates a hard line in dealing with her. He wants to give her an ultimatum: go into a treatment program, get clean and stay clean or you're out. No more free housing, and no help of any kind until you're drug free.

The father is apprehensive about the possible consequences for his daughter, but has been reluctantly convinced that his son's approach may be best for all of them, including the daughter. In spite of numerous angry discussions initiated by their son, the mother won't agree to this course of action. She is unwilling to evict the daughter, and she continues to support her daughter in many small personal ways. She sometimes spends half a day cleaning her daughter's house. When she makes meals for the father and son, she often takes a portion across the street and puts it in her daughter's refrigerator and leaves her a note encouraging her to have something to eat. She has on occasion brought laundry baskets of her daughter's clothes home and washed and folded them for her. She has become sneaky about these activities because she knows they make her son angry, and he accuses her of supporting his sister's addiction.

The authors could describe a hundred scenarios like this without having to invent a single one, simply from the experiences of participants in their family group. Each family of an addict is likely to have a similar story about their experience, and very often they have become so entrenched in dynamics such as this one that solutions seem impossible. The son complains: "As long as Mom is doing the stuff she does, nothing is going to get better." Mom replies: "I just can't see stacks of dirty clothes and an empty refrigerator without trying to help. It breaks my heart to see my daughter living like this. My son says I'm an enabler, and maybe he's right, but at least it makes me feel a little better to leave a nice plate of food in the refrigerator for her in case she comes home hungry. You should see how thin she's gotten! Sometimes she talks to me and cries and tells me how nice it is to have one person in the world who doesn't hate her!"

It will take a commitment on the part of each family member to learn new skills and to have compassion for each other to begin to develop a solution. It may take a skillful and compassionate person, an external resource, to help such a family begin to move toward healing. Compassion alone is not enough without skill and knowledge. Skill and expert knowledge are not sufficient without understanding and compassion.

It is important to start by accepting that everyone in this scenario is right, and nobody deserves to be blamed or attacked for their ideas or feelings. Even the addicted daughter is simply doing what addicts do. She is not living her life of addiction in order to make her family miserable. It's not personal. She has a serious disease of the central nervous system that impairs her judgment. She is engaging in the typical actions of the thousands of people who are afflicted with the disease of addiction.

The son's intentions are positive. He believes that not only his father and mother, but also his sister, would benefit from taking his advice. His frustration comes from feeling that he knows what is best for the family, but being totally unable to get them to accept his point of view.

The father can see the logic of his son's position and shares it to some extent, but he understands that his wife can't live with the possible negative consequences of the actions recommended by their son. He's not so sure that he could live with them either. The thought of his daughter homeless and helpless, a potential victim for every predator on the street, keeps him awake at night already. The idea of depriving her of a place of relative safety to live is something he can barely imagine. Still, if it might drive her to treatment and health, maybe he could do it.

The mother knows she can't handle it. Even if she said she would try, she knows that the first time her daughter showed up crying at her door, she would take her in.

If you feel that your Core Team has reached an impasse based on entrenched positions, and if your meetings are marked by angry accusations and recriminations, be aware that **this is not unusual for families with an addicted member. Thousands of similar families, with appropriate help, have found ways to move out of and beyond such impasses.**

How might the family in our example start making some changes? Here are a few possibilities. Remember movement in a positive direction is always possible, no matter how fixed in their points of view and how unwilling to change people may initially appear. Again, this requires commitment by the family and sometimes assistance from external resources.

First, the son might begin to see that, even if his perception of the situation is completely correct, his anger and resentment toward his parents and his sister are not helpful. If he accepts that pressuring his parents increases their already high stress level, he might agree to stop trying to push his parents to do something they aren't ready to do. He might try to step back from the situation and help his parents find smaller steps that they are willing and able to take.

A second possibility is that the son might recognize that his parents are unable to make the changes that are important to him, and he might question his reasons for continuing to live with his parents as an adult. He might decide to move into an apartment of his own, at least temporarily, until his parents come to their own decisions about how to deal with the daughter. This would change the dynamic between the parents and the daughter, as well as between the parents and son, whether or not the son continues to function as a member of the Core Team.

It could be that the mother is actually not willing, on her own initiative, to change any one single thing about the way she deals with her daughter. It's not uncommon for someone to say and feel that the current situation is unbearable, but at the same time to be unwilling to change anything at all about the way they deal with it. It's not the job of the Core Team to try to force change on an unwilling member. However, clarifying for the whole team that a particular member is unwilling or unable to change anything can itself be helpful. Acknowledging this reality can free other members to focus on themselves and identify actions they can take independently.

It is never accurate or appropriate to say: "As long as you refuse to change anything you're doing, it's hopeless. There's nothing the rest of us can do." It is important to start from where you are. Avoid all or nothing thinking. Little changes can lead to bigger changes and bring with them feelings of success rather than frustration and helplessness.

It may be that the mother, as she comes to understand the addiction process more clearly, will start to see that her actions are not truly helpful to her daughter. She may then realize that she has been providing food and laundry service to her daughter to relieve her own anxiety. She might be willing to look at the fact that when she gives money to her daughter, it just goes for more drugs. She may then agree to find a boundary that she is willing to enforce and communicate to her daughter. For example: "I can no longer give you money. It makes me feel too guilty that I'm supporting your drug habit." The ability to successfully set and maintain even one small boundary can be a real breakthrough for a team member and for the whole family. It helps break the pattern of feeling helpless in the face of addiction.

Whether the mother is willing to make any changes or not, the father is still free to manage his own relationship with his daughter, as well as with his wife and son. He might decide to take up a recreational activity he has abandoned because of the stressful situations surrounding his daughter's addiction. He might start by returning to his bowling team, which meets regularly on Tuesday nights. He will no longer allow the latest crisis with his daughter to keep him from that normal pleasant social habit. He has created a simple boundary around one of his valued activities, and has begun the process of taking back his life.

After trying this for a month, he might ask his wife to join him for a walk in the park, or find some other recreational activity they can enjoy together. A weekly outing of some sort, a movie, dinner out, or a card game with friends can be an important first step toward finding a life not dominated by worrying about the addict.

A helpful method for dealing with anger and resentment in your Core Team is to remind yourself and other members why you're a team. What brought you together? What goals do you share? Remember parents of addicts are looking to improve the quality of their own lives, protect their loved ones, and to do the right thing by their addicted child. On the basis of your love for each other and for the addicted member of your family, isn't there one small thing you can agree to do together to make your lives better?

Frustration with the Core Team Is Inevitable

If you've been able to form a team, and have identified issues to work on, and now you feel the team has become bogged down and ineffective, these may be some of the causes of your frustration:

- Someone dominates the conversations and runs roughshod over other group members.
- People talk over each other.
- There is a lack of clear focus.
- People spend much of the time talking aimlessly rather than productively addressing the issues.
- There is an inability to reach consensus and make team decisions.
- There is a lack of follow through, and no accountability for agreements made.

Following are some ground rules that may help with these problems:

- Only one person talks at a time. Make it fun by having a rain stick that gets passed to the person whose turn it is to talk.
- Agree to talk from your own feelings, needs and experiences.
- Create a safe environment by agreeing not to attack others, gossip, or make mean-spirited accusations.

Frustration with the team may be inevitable, but it is worth working through. Sometimes groups don't operate effectively because of lack of knowledge of how to conduct a meeting. In Chapter 4 we described a six step process. If your team is floundering, we suggest going back to that process, selecting or electing a temporary leader to help keep the group on task, and following that process rigorously. It's a way to get started.

There are dozens of books with titles like "How to Work Effectively in Groups," or "Effective Teams." Have a team member do some research on this issue and present ideas at the next meeting. This is a good example of addressing a team **issue** in order to more effectively address team **tasks**.

Frustration with Core Team processes and progress often have a heavy overlay of anger and resentment. Don't be surprised or disappointed if your Core Team needs to call on the Support Team to resolve such issues, especially when the Core Team is just getting started and doesn't have much experience getting past such difficult barriers.

Backsliding or Relapsing

The Core Team has been formed because its members have agreed that their current situation is unbearable and cannot be allowed to continue. That doesn't mean the team members know at the beginning how to make the situation better. That's why their decisions to take particular actions should be considered experimental and open to revision.

Team members will sometimes agree to specific actions because they think those actions are the right thing to do, or because they are desperate to change something in the hope that things will improve. It sometimes happens that after trying a specific change for a while, things don't get better and they may even get worse. Sometimes a team member who agreed to make a change finds that, when the time comes to act differently, he is unable to do so.

When these things happen, the Core Team must understand that it has not failed. The person who was not able to follow through with a Team decision is not a "bad" team member. This becomes a "failure" only if the Team isn't able to learn from the incident and move beyond it. Maybe the team was too forceful in pushing the member to agree to something that he really wasn't ready for. Maybe the member didn't completely understand how the decision was supposed to be implemented, or thought he could do something he really couldn't.

Let's go back to our example.

The mother agreed that she would no longer give her daughter money, knowing it usually gets spent on drugs.

The next week she comes to the group meeting and says: "I couldn't do it. I gave her $100." Her son asks: "How could you do that? You said you know she will just spend it on drugs." The mother is silent, but her husband answers for her. "Sue told her she's cutting back and trying to quit, but she had to have enough to taper off because she can't quit cold turkey without getting sick. She said if her mother wouldn't give her the money she'd have to find it on the street."

The one change the mother thought she could make turned out to be impossible for her. When her daughter threatened to prostitute herself for drug money, the mother saw herself as potentially responsible for that outcome, and she couldn't face the guilt.

Those of us who have lived with addiction in our immediate family are very familiar with the kind of heart-rending decisions required to begin to break the bonds established by addiction. That's why it's so important to have a good Core Team, and why it's so important for the Core Team to have access to a Support Team.

Part of the definition of the disease of addiction is that addicts will do whatever is necessary to get their drug of choice. In this example, the daughter's brain is telling her that getting the drug is not only the most important thing right now, it's the only thing that makes her life worth living. You might ask: "What kind of daughter would blackmail her mother for money by threatening to prostitute herself?" The answer is: "An addicted daughter."

The daughter knows that in her mother's value system prostitution is about the worst thing she can imagine. For the daughter, more horrifying than having sex with a stranger is not having money to satisfy her overpowering craving. Getting $100 from her mother doesn't ensure that she won't also have sex for money. It's just the most immediate and easy way to get the money she absolutely has to have right now to buy her drug.

Part of what a Support Team can do is to help a family member put a situation like this into context.

As long as the daughter is caught up in her addiction and does not acknowledge it and accept treatment, she will continue to put herself in dangerous situations. **The unhappy truth is that as long as the daughter is actively pursuing her drug of choice, there is nothing the mother or anyone else can do to protect her from the consequences.** Giving the daughter money is acting out of the belief that you can control the outcome of your daughter's addiction. You cannot.

If you can't protect your daughter from the consequences of her addiction, what can and should you do in situations like this?

We don't want to try to prescribe specific actions that a person "should" take in any specific situation. Every situation and every person is different. A good Support Team will be able to offer compassion, expertise, and guidance to family members.

On the other hand, we don't want to present situations like this and leave the reader thinking: "This is impossible. There's no right thing to do in a situation like this." So let's lay out some possible guidelines.

- It's generally not a good thing to give the addicted family member money, or allow them to manipulate you into doing things for them that they should be doing for themselves.
- The Core Team should decide how to deal with specific situations like this threat of prostitution.
- Timing is important. If you agree that giving your addicted daughter money is not advisable, you should pick the best time, place, and team member to communicate that decision to your daughter.
- The worst time is when your daughter is in the throes of her dependency and is desperate. Every addict has some periods of time when she is more or less lucid and in possession of her faculties. Pick such a time to calmly communicate your decision.
- You also have better and worse times. Pick a time when your own mental and emotional state is relatively balanced and clear to communicate the new boundary to your daughter.
- It's OK to prepare for the conversation, and it's OK to use the Core Team and/or the Support Team to help you prepare. You will need to be very clear about your own ability to

enforce a new boundary before you try to communicate it to your daughter.
- Remember, you are not preparing for a discussion. You are preparing to communicate a decision you and your Team have made. **This is not a negotiation!**

Here's an example of how you might choose to communicate this boundary to your daughter:

"Your father and I love you very much. We can see that you have been addicted to drugs for quite a while now, and we're so worried about what it's doing to you. We hope you'll admit that you have a problem and need help, and we will help you get the treatment you need. Until you go into a treatment program, we aren't going to give you any more money. We know most of it just goes for drugs. So I don't want you to ask me or your father for money any more, and I don't want to hear about how you will do this or that to get money if we don't give it to you. If you ask me for money in the future, I'll leave. I'm not willing to give you money, or to discuss this issue with you anymore. But we will find the money to help you get treatment when you're ready to accept it."

The Core Team, with the help of the Support Team, can agree to a boundary like this. But only the member who is directly involved in implementing the decision can decide whether she is ready, willing, and able to do it. In this case, the addicted daughter knows her mother is the "weak link" in the family; that's who she will go to when she is desperate for money. For that reason, nobody but the mother can effectively communicate the boundary to the daughter. She is the one who, before the boundary is communicated, has to evaluate her own conviction and courage to determine whether she can set and maintain the boundary.

Sometimes teams can come up with a plan like this and simply put it on hold. Maybe it will be months before the team member will be able to truly sign on to implementing it. That's OK. **Members should only agree to act on decisions they fully support and are emotionally able to implement.** Breaking that rule is a recipe for failure and resentment.

Manipulation

Manipulation is a complicated and many-faceted topic. In this context there are two aspects of manipulation that we want to discuss separately. They are equally important. The first and most obvious is manipulation of family members by the addicted member. The second is manipulation by Core Team members of the addict or of each other.

Manipulation by the Addict

The first thing to understand is that all addicted people manipulate. This isn't personal. It's just what addicts do as part of the set of symptoms common to their disease.

The second thing to understand is that all family members and friends are equal opportunity targets of manipulation by the addict. Remember the primary goal of the addict is to get and use their drug of choice successfully. Manipulating family members and friends is one of the most common ways addicts try to meet that goal. Manipulation is not something to be surprised or shocked about; it's part of the normal dance that occurs with the disease.

The third thing to understand is that family members will continue to be manipulated until they make a conscious decision to stop allowing this to happen, **and until they learn new skills and habits that make manipulation attempts unsuccessful.**

As long as addicts are using drugs, they will not stop trying to manipulate. Don't expect the addicted person to change this behavior. Manipulating is normal for addicts, and is often quite successful from their point of view. Family members have no control over these behaviors by the addict, but they do have or can learn to have control over their participation in the two way process of manipulation. Family members who don't understand what they can control and what they can't control spend tremendous amounts of energy trying to control the addict's manipulating behavior instead of their responses to it.

You can get a pretty good idea of how susceptible you are to manipulation by answering the following questions.

- Do you feel guilty about your loved one's addiction? Do you feel that something you did or didn't do caused or contributed to the addiction? Have you ever thought that if only you were a better husband, wife or parent, the addiction might not have happened, or the addict might accept treatment?

- When you don't believe something the addict is telling you, do you feel that you shouldn't be so cynical and distrustful? Do you feel that just this once the addict seems totally sincere, and your distrust is a violation of your relationship with him?

- Do you worry that something you said or didn't say might have triggered drug or alcohol use? Are you super-careful what you say, censoring in advance anything you think might upset or "set off" the addict? Do you "walk on egg shells" around the addict?

- When the addict tells you how hard his life is, do you automatically go into worry and distress? Do you start thinking about how you might make things better for him?

- Do you make excuses for the addict's behavior to other team members and try to elicit compassion and understanding from them on behalf of the addict?

- Do you feel chronically frustrated, angry, hopeless, stressed out, or depressed at the latest behavior or anticipated behavior by the addict?

- Do you sometimes feel that you are living as an emotional extension of the addict, without a life of your own? Does your emotional state depend more on the addict's behavior than on any other factor in your life?

The more of these questions you answered "Yes," the more susceptible you may be to allowing yourself to be manipulated by the addict. Reducing your susceptibility to manipulation requires family members to develop some "unnatural" skills:

- Saying no to the heartfelt pleas of your beloved child;
- Not trusting the most sincere promises of your loved one;
- Developing boundaries as tools to prevent emotional blackmail by the addict;
- Believing what you see rather than what you would like to believe;
- Regaining elements of your life that you have abandoned;
- Recognizing that feeling sorry for and attempting to rescue the addict can be a reaction to manipulation, not true compassion;
- Avoiding responses to the addict based on anger and resentment;
- Giving up the illusion that you can control outcomes for the addict;
- Understanding that maintaining boundaries may feel like cold and uncaring behavior on your part, but can be one of the most loving and caring things you can do for the addict and for yourself.

These are not easy skills to learn, and they are extremely difficult to maintain without support. But it is possible to learn to apply them little by little. Working with your Core Team and Support Team as described in the last three chapters makes it possible to recognize when you are acting within the boundaries you've established, and when you are being manipulated.

Manipulation of the Addict by the Core Team

Dealing with manipulation of the addict by Core Team members is a little more challenging, because it requires us to examine our own thoughts and actions rather than those of the addict.

Here are three warning signals that you are verging on manipulation of the addict:

- Your focus is mainly on the addict and not on the entire family.
- Your discussions and plans are aimed at creating particular outcomes **for the addict;**
- The specific boundaries you are discussing or planning are primarily driven by anger or resentment at the addict, or they are punitive.

Families and friends beginning this process often have been trying to control too many things in the addict's life at the expense of their own lives because they have been so anxious about the addict. When a Core Team starts to work, the tendency is to continue this focus on the addict's life.

In the scenario we have been using as an example in this chapter, the parents might agree to stop providing money and free housing to their addicted daughter unless she goes into a treatment program. Why would they agree to do this? Perhaps because they think that under the threat of homelessness, their daughter will see the light and begin a program to cure her addiction. A good Support Team would recognize this as an attempt to manipulate the addict, to try to create a particular outcome for the addict.

Setting boundaries as a way to try to make the addict change a particular behavior is a very understandable tendency, but it is rarely effective. One reason is that addicts tend to be far better at manipulation than their families and friends. The whole purpose and goal of their lives, as they understand them, depends on their ability to successfully manipulate others. As the date set for the eviction draws closer, the daughter will pull out all stops to create guilt and anxiety in her parents. In this case, the mother already knows that she can't follow through on the threat, and this is not likely to be missed by the daughter.

What is the family's motivation in establishing a particular boundary? This is a critical issue. The action or boundary contemplated must be intended to improve the quality of life for the rest of the family. It may or may not involve the addict directly.

A key issue with addiction and families is whether or not to allow the addict to continue to live in the family home. There is no one answer or correct approach to this question. When it is considered by the Core Team, it is important to refer back to the question: why would we want to do this? **Is it**

because living with the addict makes it impossible for the rest of the family to have an acceptable quality of life? Or is it to try to force the addict to change his behavior and perhaps seek treatment?

Does the Core Team want to set a boundary about lending the addict a family car because they have some other use for the car, because they are concerned about liability issues, or to punish the addict for not using the car responsibly?

Is the team taking actions to control their own environment and their own reactions to the addict, or are they trying to create boundaries that fence in the addict and try to control the addict's actions?

Whose life are you trying to manage? Certainly the life of the addict and the lives of family members and friends are intertwined, but it is usually possible to figure out the answer to this question as it relates to a particular action discussed by the Core Team. Practice, plus the input of a good Support Team, will make this easier.

We have said that addicts tend to respond only to pain. Without pain they will not be motivated to seek help with their addiction. We encourage families and friends to allow the addicted person they love to experience the consequences of their addiction without trying to cushion them or save them.

However, it is not the job of the family or the Core Team to create pain for the addict in the hope of driving them into treatment! Addicts create plenty of pain for themselves. We have seen families kick their adult child out of the house thinking that this will make them go into treatment, and then be devastated and guilty when the child does not go into treatment but ends up on the street.

There are no simple solutions to such situations. **If you choose not to allow your addicted spouse or adult child to continue to live in your house, it should be done to make your own life better, to protect your environment, not to punish or manipulate the addict.** You are simply controlling your environment and determining how you will react to the addictive behavior. If this results in the addicted person going into treatment or creating some alternative sobriety plan, that's great, but the expectation that they will should not be the basis for the action.

Stopping enabling behaviors simply allows the addict to experience the natural consequences of addiction, and they will deal with it as a normal consequence of their addiction, not as a consequence of the family's manipulative decision to cause pain.

Making decisions designed primarily to protect your family's well-being, and not to affect outcomes for the addict follows some basic principles discussed in previous chapters:

- **We have to learn to give up trying to control outcomes for the addict**. This doesn't mean abandoning them. The outcome for the addicted person can only be determined by the addict, not by you.

- **Addiction does not respond to logical thought, but only to experience**. Allow the addict to experience whatever they create in their own lives. When we rescue our addicted family members from the consequences of their behavior, we prevent them from experiencing the consequences of their addiction.

CHAPTER 7. BUILDING RELATIONSHIPS WITH ADDICTS: TRUST AND COMMUNICATION.

If a member of your family is actively using, you can still build a healthier relationship with them than you might think possible.

Relationships within the family are strained by the added pressures created by addiction, so developing a strategy to ease this tension becomes necessary for everyone's well-being. The following three skills, which we have discussed at length in previous chapters, are designed to help family members work together to deal with those pressures:

- **Finding and using appropriate support;**
- **Working effectively as a team; and**
- **Creating and maintaining boundaries.**

These skills all involve family members, but not the addict, working together as a team.

There is an equally important set of skills that are focused directly on the relationships of family members with the addict. Those skills are:

- **Managing loss of trust; and**
- **Improving communication with the addict and other family members.**

These skills will be the focus of this chapter.

Managing loss of trust.

As you work toward improving your relationship with an addicted family member, you will discover that your interactions with them begin to look and feel a lot different than you might have anticipated. One of the first things to learn is the paradox that not trusting them is a good thing. **Being untrustworthy is an inevitable and predictable result of addiction**. Learning to understand this and to work with it rather than feeling angry and hurt at every instance of untrustworthiness is an important milestone. It is good when you are not surprised to find that the addict has lied to you. It means that you are starting to see the addict more realistically. **Of course they are lying. That's what addicts do.** This acceptance doesn't mean your values need to change, or that you now think lying is OK. It means you are facing the facts and creating a basis for dealing appropriately with the untrustworthiness.

It is normal for family members to get caught up in the words and promises that addicts make. It seems easier to relate to them from a memory of a time in the past when we could count on their word than to face that someone we love can no longer be counted on to be truthful. We must learn to simply watch their behavior. **The adage "Actions speak louder than words" should be something we imprint in our minds when listening to an addict**.

A critical aspect of managing the loss of trust is developing the skill to detach emotionally from a situation and give yourself permission to do nothing instead of immediately reacting to any statement the addict makes. Imagine yourself taking a step back to just observe rather than act. If you are constantly reacting to the addict, you are not learning. You will just grow more frustrated and perceive yourself as increasingly powerless. This may lead you to feel discouraged, angry, and resentful.

The fact that addiction severely undermines your trust in the addict should not be used against them. It is not helpful to challenge them with statements such as "I don't believe you" or "You're a liar." It is important for you to learn to manage your own behavior, develop a healthy skepticism, and just observe what they do over time. It may be helpful to develop a set of responses that reflect this attitude: "Let's see how it works out;" or "Sounds OK to me;" or "Go for it." Don't create expectations; wait for actions.

Rebuilding trust is a gradual process. We build trust with our addicted family member the same way we build trust with anyone. When their words match their actions on a consistent basis, our trust level automatically rises.

What is disarming for many families is that when addicted family members promise something, they may sound totally sincere, and they may even mean what they say at the moment. Inevitably the family feels let down when the addict doesn't show up or follow through. The truth is that addicts can't trust themselves to consistently follow through with plans for the future. Even though you want to be able to trust the addict, it is healthier for everyone if you do not. **Being able to comfortably not trust the addict is the goal**. It is best not to take their being untrustworthy personally. Their thought processes have been warped by the need to keep using.

Untrustworthy behavior is predictable and usually falls into one of two categories: **the conscious deception of others; or self deception.**

Conscious deception is most often used to manipulate a specific response from you. The purpose is generally to avoid experiencing the negative consequences of addiction. For example, the addict may request money to buy food, but the money is actually used for drugs or alcohol. Or the addict may ask to borrow your car to go on a non-existent job interview, when the real plan is to make a drug connection.

Self deception is usually related to plans that addicts believe they will follow through on but don't or can't. For example, the addict may tell you about his plans to get a college degree when in fact he is unable to stay sober for more than a couple of weeks at a time, and his brain is so muddled that he can't manage his own finances. This topic may trigger hopeful feelings in you. It may match up with a life-long goal you've held for your family member. Don't let an ingrained pattern of thinking overpower the realistic part of you that knows this may be a fine goal at some later date, but without a serious period of sobriety it isn't realistic. You don't help an addict by participating in their fantasy life.

If you see that the addict is going to get into a typical long discussion about unrealistic future plans, it's OK to just say "Let's see how it turns out," and move on to something you need to do. Unfortunately many times families buy into the self-deception because they are eager to accept what would appear to be reasonable goals stated by the addict. In reality these goals are just words, and family members would be better off not to put faith in the words of the addict.

Reserve your trust until it is warranted by consistent positive action by the addict. This is necessary for your own emotional survival.

It isn't easy to accept that someone you love repeatedly violates your core values. As you start to understand that this is how addicted people think and behave, you will be able to step back from these situations when they occur and not fall into emotional booby traps that leave you feeling drained and helpless. An important marker that will indicate you have made a big step forward is that instead of getting hooked into the promises your family member makes, you are able to just observe their behavior and see if the behavior matches the words.

Addicted people can't see beyond their own needs. Their thought processes are distorted by their mental obsession and physical craving for their drug of choice. It is important for you to require that they earn your trust back by following through on their words with appropriate behavior. It is important to base your own behavior toward the addict on this understanding.

Improving Communication with the Addict and Other Family Members.

Before you begin to read this section, we need to make one important point: if the addict in your family is violent or inclined toward physical or extreme verbal violence, the skills and tools we describe in this section will not be useful until the issue of violence has been addressed. See Chapter 10, Section B on violent behavior.

Addicts need accurate information. Give consistent and non-judgmental messages that you love them; you believe they have a serious medical condition; you want them to get help; and you will be supportive of them in their recovery. Communicate these four messages in a calm, neutral manner. Practice giving these messages over and over again without anger or blame and without regard for the addict's rejection.

Developing a clear and straightforward communication style with addicted family members will assist you in establishing healthy emotional boundaries between them and yourself. This is an essential task if you are to improve your relationship with them. Establishing and maintaining healthy boundaries will be primarily your task. Addicts are not capable of doing this while they are still using or are in the early stages of recovery. They are so absorbed in their own reality that they often don't recognize when they cross boundaries and cause problems for other people.

Clear communication is an important aspect of all healthy relationships. Addiction will create special challenges in this area. Drug and alcohol addiction have a profound effect on the brain and reduce the ability to make rational decisions and to follow through on tasks of daily living. This has a direct impact on how you are able to communicate with the addict.

In the following short discussions, we have tried to gather together some ideas that address recurring situations related to communicating with addicted family members.

Self-Talk.

Improving your communication skills in the difficult environment created by addiction begins with your own self talk. Pay attention to what you are communicating to yourself in your own mind. You may find yourself thinking things like: "Where have I gone wrong"; "Nothing I say makes a dent"; "I shouldn't have said that; it just sets him off." Remind yourself that you didn't cause your loved one's addiction, you can't control it, and you can't cure it. Recognize the importance of forgiving your past mistakes. We all make mistakes. Yours did not cause the addiction or the latest binge.

Self-reproach weakens your ability to speak clearly or to take effective action. When you find yourself engaging in negative thoughts, you can deliberately offset them by switching to positive self-talk. Tell yourself the truth: "I can't undo the past. It's gone and that's OK"; "In this moment I am learning to become a more skillful communicator"; "I am taking control of my own mind and training it to support my efforts to improve how I communicate."

Worrying thoughts like "He won't live much longer if he keeps doing what he's doing" can be countered with statements like "None of us knows the future," or "He's in God's hands." Self-blaming thoughts like "I was so preoccupied with my own problems that I didn't realize how hard our divorce was on my son" can be replaced with the conscious acknowledgment that you did the very best you could both for yourself and for your son.

Avoiding Negative Conversations.

As you begin to pay attention to what thoughts recur in your head, you will also notice that some types of external conversations upset you. Talk that increases your anxiety level is counter-productive. Just because the addict wants to talk to you doesn't mean you have to listen. Think of yourself as an actor who needs to learn some good exit lines, and remove yourself from the drama.

If the addict wants to tell you "bar horror stories" about how much they drank, how drunk they were, how they got into a fight, etc., you can simply say: "It's not good for me to hear about these things." You can change the subject to something of interest to you, or you can go do something somewhere else. You know that hearing these things causes you distress, and that listening gives positive attention to negative behavior.

Dealing with an addict can produce rage on the scale of a volcanic eruption. Venting at the addict in hopes of getting through to them simply enables them to focus on you as the problem rather than seeing their substance abuse as the problem. To counter the natural tendency to erupt at the addict, it's necessary to train yourself to step back and use alternatives.

Perhaps the most important skill is learning how not to react at all to provocative behavior. Family members sometimes believe that they have to respond in some way to whatever the addict says or does. In fact, it's almost never productive to try to have a serious conversation with someone while they are actively drunk or high. It's better to simply say: "We'll talk about that when you're sober." Or "I don't want to talk to you now."

You have the power to limit how much and under what circumstances you are available to the addict in your family. Casually saying "I'm going to go fix myself a snack," or "I think the washer just went off," you can remove yourself from the environment of negative conversations. Learning that you don't have to listen to someone who is drunk or high, or who wants to engage you in negative or unproductive conversations, is an important survival skill. If you have a Support Group, they may be able to help you develop strategies to protect yourself from the verbal onslaught.

"I Messages."

These are simple statements that let people know who you are, what you like and don't like, what you want and don't want, and how you feel. Practicing "I Messages" counters our natural tendency to say harsh or negative things about someone else instead of simply identifying how we are affected by someone's behavior. Here are a few sets of "I messages" and "You messages" to help you see the difference.

YOU: "Your friend Steve is a drunk and a thief. Don't ever bring him here again."

I: "I don't want you to bring Steve here again. I'm not comfortable having him in my house."

YOU: "Shut up! You're drunk and crazy and I can't stand listening to you."

I: "I don't want to talk to you when you've been drinking."

YOU: "If you come home drunk in the middle of the night one more time, you're out of here."

I: "I need to have the house quiet after 10 p.m. If you can't get home before 10, I want you to find some other place to spend the night."

More samples of "I messages":

"I want you to know that I love you."

"I'm not willing to lie to your boss for you."

"I feel sad that we don't go to church together anymore."

This is not as simple as it sounds. It's easy to fall into attacks or accusations disguised as "I messages." Any sentence that starts out "I feel like you..." is problematic. "I feel like you never listen to me" is an accusation, not an "I message."

It helps to identify to yourself exactly what your feelings are before trying to disclose them. Are you angry, sad, hopeful, fearful, etc? And what do you want to accomplish by sharing this information about your feelings with the listener? Addicts usually lack the clarity of mind and emotional stability to provide the understanding and support you may be seeking. This is why we emphasize the need to find support from some other source.

You need safe outlets for talking about how you are feeling and what you need. Exposing your vulnerability to the addicted member of your family just provides openings for manipulation. **It is the nature of the disease of addiction that the addict can't attend to someone else's needs.** The practicing addict's needs are all-consuming for them. This same person may well have been a primary source of emotional support for you in the past, which makes it hard to acknowledge and accept how unavailable to you he or she is in the present.

Addiction changes relationships beyond recognition. Our tendency is to continue to try to relate to the addict as he was before addiction took over his personality. It takes time and effort to accept that the cunning and manipulative person before you is who you are dealing with now. The grief of losing the relationship you trusted and valued is too heavy to bear alone; it helps to share it with people who understand what you are going through.

Repetition.

In normal relationships and normal conversations, we try to avoid repetition. In communicating with people with addictions, repetition is your friend. There are several reasons for this.

The most important reason repetition is a useful tool is that practicing addicts are very persistent. Like a child who responds to everything you say with another "Why," an addict tends to feel he is successfully manipulating you as long as you feel obligated to continue to engage in conversation. You may have dozens of things you need to be doing; the addict typically has only one thing he needs: to wear you down until you agree to do whatever it is he wants at that moment.

Let's use one of the examples from the "I Messages" section above. You're practicing using an "I Message" when you say to your addicted family member: "I don't want you to bring Steve here again." The predictable response is not "OK. I won't." More likely it will be a belligerent: "What do you have against Steve? You don't even know him." Going into all the reasons you don't want Steve in your house will inevitably lead to a long argument about Steve's virtues and vices. This will not serve you. You know Steve is someone who shares your family member's addiction and you don't want him in your house. It's OK to repeat, several times if necessary: "Steve's not somebody I want in my house. Don't bring him here again or invite him over." If your family member persists, you can refuse to continue the conversation: "I don't want to argue with you about it. I don't want Steve in my house."

Rationality is irrelevant in conversations with a practicing addict; repetition can take its place. Some addicts love to engage family members in rambling, maudlin conversations, often when the exhausted family member only wants to get some sleep. It's not helpful to humor the addict. It's OK to say: "I don't want to talk to you now; I'm going to go to bed (or to do something, or to go somewhere else)." Again, the addict is not likely to find this acceptable, and may insist that he really needs to talk to you about incredibly meaningful thoughts and feelings. It's not your job to substitute for the addict's relationships he lost as a result of addiction. Just cut him off calmly, repeat your message, and then leave him.

To use this tool effectively, you will need to train yourself to avoid the subtle lures the addict will put in front of you to keep you engaged in the conversation. Here's an example of the use of guilt and pathos that an addict can use. The addict returns home after the bars have closed or after getting kicked out of the local bar and persistently attempts to engage in long, emotional discussions on various topics. A suitable response would be: "I'm not willing to talk to you when you've been drinking." The addict will try to play on your emotions: "I can't talk to you when I'm sober. I have some things I really need to talk to you about, and I need to do it now." Don't bite. Just say: "I'm sorry you can't talk to me when you're sober. That's something we can work on later when you haven't been drinking."

Addicts are masters at knowing what hook is likely to keep you engaged. You have to become equally masterful at avoiding the hook and calmly repeating your position. Family members tend to feel obligated to respond to everything the addict in the family says or does. Observe the ways the addict gets you into arguments or meaningless discussions. Use your support resources to strategize how you will deal with the situation when it comes up again.

It can be very useful to develop straightforward statements that you can use whenever the situation calls for them:

- I don't want to talk about that now.
- I'm not willing to talk to you when you're drunk (or high). Let's talk about that another time.
- That's not something I can do anything about.
- There's no point talking about that now. You'd need to be sober or straight for a while before you'd be ready for that.
- No. I've already told you that you can't use my car any more. When you've got six months of sobriety I'll be willing to discuss this again.
- No. I've already told you I won't give you money any more. Please don't ask again.
- You have a serious problem with drugs (or alcohol) and I really would like for you to go into a treatment program. Until you do, there's not much I can do to help you.

Don't expect that your loved one will agree with or accept your message. If the addict protests or argues, don't get sucked into the argument. Just repeat the message you want the addicted person to hear, and don't take rejection or lack of interest in the message personally. Your consistent, calm, non-judgmental responses are the best you can do. Your addicted family member may not respond positively or at all, but they may remember the message at some later time.

As long as what you say is honest in terms of your own ideas and values, and is respectful to the addict in your family, you are communicating as effectively as you can. Whether your messages fall on deaf ears or are eventually received and acted on is beyond your control.

Having people who support you in trying new approaches is invaluable. For any of us, changing our habits of mind and how we respond to stressful situations is not easy. People use expressions like, "Rome wasn't built in a day" to remind themselves that real change takes time. Members of a Support Group can sometimes recognize and acknowledge progress when we are discouraged that the "problem" hasn't been solved. Their encouragement can help us stay focused on what we are trying to accomplish.

Your ability to stay calm and consistent conveys the message that you are sane, reliable, and trustworthy. It makes it more likely that you will be heard and taken seriously.

CHAPTER 8. RECOVERY AND RELAPSE.

When people think about relapse they picture the addict starting to use again after a period of being drug and alcohol free. We've discovered that family members of the addict experience their own relapses as well.

Relapse for an addict is clear; they start using again. There are usually warning signs before this happens. If the addict has developed a strong support system while sober, he can use it to short circuit the relapse and get back on track.

The process is similar with family members who have learned new and healthier ways to relate to an addict. Even those who have worked at becoming less focused on controlling the addict, have reduced their own level of isolation, and have developed a support system can experience relapse.

Some signs that families are heading for relapse are that they are:

- Experiencing increased levels of anxiety and feelings of apprehension, "walking on eggshells."
- Putting the addict's needs above your own, causing a noticeable decline in self-care. Not making dental or doctor appointments for yourself when you should. Not getting enough exercise. Not being able to get a good night's sleep.
- Putting yourself in the role of the addict's counselor and taking on their problems as your own.

- Making their sobriety your business, not theirs.
- Ceasing to use your support system. Isolating and not talking about the stressful feelings you are experiencing.

Both types of relapse are discouraging, but can be reversed. Family members' relapses can be shortened in both seriousness and duration. This can be accomplished by developing your ability to recognize rising anxiety levels and old behavior patterns re-emerging, and then using this insight to reconnect with support systems. These outside support networks are very valuable. They help us get back on track when things begin to go haywire.

Families can relapse while the addict remains clean and sober. The following is an example of this.

Luis and Maria have a son who began using ice, marijuana and alcohol in high school. He displayed increasingly unpredictable and destructive behavior. The parents were at a loss about how to deal with the chaos he created and began seeking outside help. While they were getting support for themselves something happened to their son that frightened him and he suddenly moved to another state. While he was living away from home he stopped using drugs and got a job. They were encouraged by the phone conversations they had with him and believed that he had turned his life around. They had been working on turning their lives around as well. They began taking better care of themselves. They talked more openly with each other about their thoughts and feelings. They continued participating in a support group for themselves.

After their son had been living away for more than a year they received a call from him that he wanted to come home for a visit. They were both excited and scared at the prospect of having him in their home again. As his arrival time drew closer their anxiety level kept escalating. Old memories of how much stress they were under when he was living at home and using dominated their thinking and emotions. Time seemed to collapse for them. They weren't able to separate the teenager that caused them so much grief from the young man returning home. They had learned about healthier ways to relate to an addict while their son was away, but once he was actually back in their environment they slipped into full relapse. Even though their son came home clean and sober the family interacted with him, and each other, as though he was still using. They were anxious about where he was, who he was with, and what time he came home at night. The parents started blaming each other for the tension in the house and getting into heated arguments. They relapsed because, when their sober addict visited them, fear and anxiety overwhelmed their emotions and good judgment, leading them to behave as they had in the past.

Luckily, they knew they were in trouble and went to their support group to get a reality check. Being able to talk openly about what they were going through with a group of people they trusted helped them get a clearer perspective on what was happening to them. They were able to identify things they could do to handle the situation better. With the help of the group they were able to end this first visit in a way that left them all feeling hopeful for better contacts in the future. This situation created a learning experience for the whole family. Realizing that an event that initially was so troubling could be worked through in a way that left them all feeling stronger as a family turned a negative situation into a positive experience. This is an example of how stressful situations can provide an opportunity for family members to gain new perspectives, show greater respect for one another and grow closer together. This kind of growth is built on being open to new ideas and willingness to change old behavior patterns. Family relationships can become a source of pleasure not pain.

What this family experienced is similar to the combination of hopeful expectation and fearful anxiety that many families go through when an addicted family member returns from a residential treatment program.

Many families feel a huge sense of relief when the addict begins a program of sobriety. This is an outcome that they have hoped and often prayed for; they think their problem has been solved. However important this step might be, it doesn't change the fact that recovery, for the family as well as for the addict, is a life-long process. **The recovery process has its own challenges and requires learning some new skills.**

Managing expectations is an important skill. Thinking that things will return to being as they were in the good old days before substance abuse became a problem is a recipe for disappointment.

Years of substance abuse take a very real toll on the addict and the family. The addict's getting clean and sober is just the beginning of a long climb back to what may remain an impaired functioning level. However, it is possible to engage in the recovery process in a way that results in family relationships being better than they ever were before addiction became an issue.

Yearning for an imagined ideal past becomes an obstacle to successfully dealing with the issues recovery presents for both the family and the recovering addict. An example of this kind of thinking is a remark made by the former wife of an addict who now has many years clean and sober. She said, "Eddie used to be a lot of fun." She was remembering the years when Eddie was able to drive himself to work endless hours and make a lot of money by staying high on cocaine. Those were fun days for her: sex, drugs and rock and roll. She had lost the connection to how that same drug use resulted in his ever crazier behavior, their subsequent financial problems and the breakup of their family. The ex-husband she doesn't see as being much fun anymore is still clean and sober and happily married to someone else.

Another challenge family members face is feeling left out and ignored when their newly sober addict starts attending AA or NA meetings. Some programs require 90 meetings in the first 90 days of sobriety. Recovering addicts are encouraged to get a sponsor and call them every day. These activities take up a lot of the recovering addict's time and attention. You may have believed that once your loved one was sober you would feel closer to them, but instead find yourself distanced by the new experiences they are having, and resenting the new friends they are making. You may find that their primary sharing is with their sponsor and others who can relate to their struggles with recovery. That is why we can't emphasize enough the importance of having developed a strong support system of your own to help you through this difficult period.

Although everyone's recovery is unique, general patterns and stages in the recovery process have been identified. Having concrete information about the typical trajectory of substance abuse recovery is helpful. It gives family members a more realistic view of what living with a recovering addict is like.

You've learned that an addict's thinking and behavior in the active use stage of addiction is predictable and not personal. This same dynamic exists in recovery. The addict experiences changes in energy levels and moods and other challenges at predictable stages, and these are not unique, not personal, and not about you. They are part of the recovery process. Being able to recognize and understand them for what they are makes it easier to view the process with some objectivity. Having correct information can help you continue to support the addict's recovery while maintaining healthy boundaries.

The Substance Abuse and Mental Health Services Administration of the U.S. Department of Health (SAMHSA) has developed a model of the recovery process that we will present here with minor modifications.

The first stage, **Withdrawal,** occurs when an addict is detoxing from alcohol or drug use. It lasts about two weeks (longer if recovering from methamphetamine dependence). When a chemically dependent person stops using they will go through some form of withdrawal. This may range from minor physical reactions to serious life threatening symptoms that require hospitalization, depending on the type of drug and level of use. At this stage the addict is chemically depleted. They don't have enough "feel good" chemicals in their brain. Their serotonin and dopamine levels are low and often calcium and other important nutrients are also depleted. During this phase you will likely observe irritability, low energy, anxiety, depression, anger, insomnia, cravings, loneliness, resentment and distrust. Being around someone in this unstable state is difficult, so you can see why detoxing in a facility where people are trained to deal with addiction is desirable. **Keep in mind that detox (getting the drugs out of the addict's body) is not treatment. It's an opportunity to begin treatment**.

The Early Abstinence or **Honeymoon period** generally occurs in the month following withdrawal. The body is manufacturing more dopamine and serotonin. The brain is getting a wake-up call. This results in a higher energy level with the addict wanting to make up for lost time. Even though the addict is feeling better and probably looking better, their brain is still in recovery mode, making it hard for them to be realistic about their priorities. This is a time when they are likely to feel overconfident, that they have been cured, or that perhaps they aren't an addict after all, so it's safe to start using again. They are vulnerable to people, places, things, times and emotional states that can trigger relapse. Some family members may not be willing to modify their own life style in deference to the newly clean and sober addict, while others may want to make some changes to show support for the addict new to sobriety. For example, if holidays are especially difficult for the addict, you may want to scale back your celebrations, or you may not want to drink alcohol in front of the addict, since the smell of alcohol can be a strong trigger. Being able to discuss these issues openly with your team and either come to a consensus or agree to disagree is continuing the work of maintaining a respectful dialogue in your home, and acknowledging that sobriety presents a new set of challenges.

During the honeymoon phase family members need to be wary of getting swept up in the addict's enthusiasm for their miraculous transformation. They often have grand plans for restarting their life, going back to school, beginning a new business venture, etc. Unfortunately, the energy they are feeling at this point isn't likely to last. What they are feeling and what you are observing is a short-lived phase. The addict still has a lot of work to do. Family members don't need to be discouraging, but they do need to remember to observe behavior, stay grounded, and maintain their boundaries.

If the addict tries to do too much too soon it will trigger anxiety and increase the risk of relapse. If you buy into their being "cured" and don't maintain your boundaries you are putting yourself at risk of relapse.

The SAMHSA model labels the third stage of recovery protracted abstinence, or **The Wall.** The lovely surge of chemicals from the honeymoon period drops. The brain is trying to stabilize and locate its new normal. Recovering addicts are often depressed, sluggish, irritable and unable to experience pleasure.

Coping with having someone around the house who has insomnia at night, sleeps during the day, lacks concentration, and feels bored and hopeless is especially difficult for spouses who have been looking forward to their newly sober mate being a real companion, helping them with the kids, pulling their weight around the house, or getting a job. It's normal to feel anger and resentment after living with an addict and then winding up with someone who is unsupportive of you and your needs once they get sober.

It is hard not to take their lack of ability to come up with much personally. You may begin to start thinking that you prefer the way they were when they were using, or you may live in fear that they will start using again. In either case, if you begin to feel guilty because you are having some negative thoughts and feelings, don't share them with a shaky, recovering addict; use your support team.

This is a period of emotional instability and a difficult one to navigate. The addict can be doing all the right things and still feel lousy. It is his first look at the long haul of recovery, which means dealing with the realities of life and all its challenges without the escape that drug use has provided in the past. During this period he also faces a variety of issues such as loss of motivation, learning to experience pleasure, dealing with emotions, handling finances, engaging in normal conversations. These are things we often take for granted, but they are life-skills that may have been lost to addiction.

The recovering addict may become impatient with what feels like a lack of progress and use this as a justification for relapsing. Family members can be torn between wanting to be patient and encouraging and being angry and fed up with living with someone who is in a constant funk. This period, the Wall, typically lasts for four or five months from when the addict got clean and sober. It is a difficult time for everyone in the family, and hopefully you will all keep in mind that "this too shall pass." The possibility of relapse is high during this phase so it is critical for the addict to stay connected to AA, NA, or whatever support system is available to them. They need reassurance that the emotional ups and downs they are experiencing are normal and not a sign of failure.

You are at risk for relapse as well, if you isolate and stop using your teams. Don't be afraid to ask for help from whatever resources you have developed.

The next stage of recovery, the **Adjustment** phase, is when the recovering addict begins experiencing normal emotions. The physiological aspects of drug use have receded, but underlying issues such as a lack of realistic goals, guilt and shame over past failures or mistakes, or relationship problems still need to be addressed.

Recovering addicts may court relapse by hanging out with old drinking buddies, going to places where they used in the past, not attending AA meetings, and being unwilling to deal with emotional issues.

Family members may court relapse by becoming too complacent. The desire to just be the way we were before all this happened is strong. It is easy to be seduced by fanciful thoughts of the future or a rosily remembered past. Staying in the present, keeping committed to having family meetings, maintaining your boundaries, and continuing to take good care of yourself are just as important now as when you first began to deal with having an addict in the family. You still do. Enjoy that things are better, but know that the progress you've made needs to be continuously nurtured and protected.

The last stage of recovery is called **Resolution**. Don't let the name fool you. This is not the end of the road or a signal that the issue has been resolved. The addict is coming to grips with the idea of never being able to use again, and learning to manage life clean and sober, one day at a time.

Family members have to accept that the addict in their family has been changed by drug use and all of their lives have been altered by what they have experienced. Their expectations may need to be adjusted as they too learn to live life one day at a time. They also need to continue using their support systems as an important aspect of maintaining a healthier life.

Recovering from addiction is a lifetime process. It is more usual for addicts to reach some stage on the recovery continuum and then relapse, than to stop using and stay stopped. The repetitive nature of relapse gives families an opportunity to look at how they've reacted during past cycles and alter their own responses the next time around.

Family members' emotional wellbeing must not be allowed to be in the hands of the addict, who has a great deal of difficulty managing his own emotional life. Families will experience emotional ups and downs, wins and disappointments. They become stronger by facing the challenges addiction presents and by developing clarity of purpose and intention. With the help of supportive resources, they can learn to manage their own lives more independently of the addict, resulting in relapses occurring less frequently.

A relapse is a series of events and choices that ultimately lead back to unhealthy behaviors. The key to preventing or recovering from a relapse is your ability to use your support system. Develop your support system now. Work toward building trust with people who are struggling with similar issues. Don't allow shame or fear to prevent you from finding the right people to be around. Having this support is the key to the recovery process for both you and the addict in your family.

CHAPTER 9. ADDICTION IN MINORS.

Parents who have a teenager who is showing signs of substance abuse are often frightened that their worst fears have come true. When they bring the subject up with their youth, they get responses like: "I just had a few beers with my friends; they all drink a lot more than I do." Or "Everyone I know smokes pot. It's not an addictive drug; it's medically approved."

When parents bring up the topic of drug use, arguments often ensue, usually with the teens accusing the parents of being uptight, out of touch with how things are today, not wanting them to have any fun, etc. These confrontations can escalate over time, with the parents becoming angrier and more anxious and the youth becoming more aggressive or withdrawn.

This dynamic of confrontational or pained accusations resulting in hostile or sullen denial is difficult to change without getting help from an outside source. The level of emotion generated by the fear of having a child spinning out of control intensifies the need to find someone to talk to who understands addiction and has some emotional distance from the problem.

It is tempting to throw your hands up in despair and say, "I can't get through to that kid." But this is not the time to abdicate your parental authority. It is the time to identify all possible sources of support and use them. When you are under a lot of stress it is understandable to feel helpless and hopeless, but there is always something you can do.

I want to share some of my own experiences with you, because they have much in common with what many families have experienced or are experiencing now.

When my stepson was in high-school he started going camping with his buddies on weekends. He was becoming more evasive, and his eyes and manner suggested to me that he was getting stoned. My husband and I discussed my observations and concerns. We then contacted social workers in agencies that dealt with problem teens, and asked several of these sources, "What child psychologist has the best reputation for helping teenagers?" We checked to see if he accepted our insurance and was able to take on a new patient.

Armed with a plan my husband and I sat our son down. We told him our concerns and that we wanted to go as a family and talk with someone more objective than we were able to be about what was going on. Our son agreed to go with us and meet the psychologist. The doctor initially talked to the three of us, and then asked to talk to our son alone. Luckily, they hit it off and our son decided he was willing to keep seeing this doctor on his own. He continued counseling for several months until he and the therapist agreed it was no longer necessary. We were very fortunate to have found the right person to help us and that our son was receptive to getting help. This is not always the case. Often there is difficulty either in finding the right resource or resistance on the part of the youth in accepting treatment.

What I learned from this experience was that taking action early on before a problem escalates gives you a better chance of having a positive outcome.

Many years later when a relative of mine sent his son to live with us, I encountered both of these problems—-a much more resistant youth and greater difficulty accessing services. This boy had been expelled from school in 7th grade for bringing pot on campus. By the time he came to live with us at age 15 he had been abusing drugs and alcohol for four years and had only earned 1 high school credit. He had spent years defying his parents' demands, and had passive resistance down to a fine science. He was uncooperative, but not openly defiant. He was self-destructive, inhaling solvent and glue fumes, cutting himself and acting out in ways that brought him trouble with authority figures. He resented his parents for sending him away to live in a state far from his home, with relatives he hadn't seen for several years.

When I felt overwhelmed, I would picture the open, loving, sweet child he had been years earlier. That memory sustained me as I dealt with the school calling me about his failing grades, the police calling me to come pick him up drunk, the truant officer coming to my home, etc. Holding the vision of his kind-hearted nature while dealing with the chaos he created was essential for me. It allowed me to remain compassionate toward his suffering. I could see that he did not trust adults, and had little ability to articulate his feelings. He was constantly acting out his anger and frustration, abusing drugs and alcohol to escape a reality he did not understand and was ill equipped to handle.

Finding services for him was more difficult than I anticipated. Part of the problem initially was that I couldn't enroll him in school until his parents had documents drawn up making me his legal guardian. During the interim I was able to find a psychologist for him to talk to. He would go with me to keep the appointment, but spent the time staring at the floor. I still took him every week. The wily psychologist had some interesting little things around her office near where he sat that captured his attention. She would make subtle comments about them and engage him in this very non-threatening way. He was willing to see her. He was lonely and she was an interesting, safe presence. He never bared his soul to her or talked about his troubles in depth, but this was a start. I think he was getting a sense that there are safe havens in this world and that they are available to him. This was the first crack in the tough protective shell he had created for himself. He was able to tell her that he had a sister and a dog back home, but not that his parents had just gotten divorced, his dad was terminally ill, and he didn't know if they would ever let him come back home.

We adults are often so caught up in our own struggles that it is hard to see beyond the tough façade young people present and realize how much stress they are dealing with and how vulnerable they feel.

Once I was able to get him enrolled in high school a new set of problems emerged. He didn't turn in assignments even when he had completed them, he skipped classes, and was disruptive in class when he did attend. I became a familiar face at the school, and met with his academic counselor. We got him placed in classes better suited to his needs, but he did not take advantage of the help they offered. I met with the substance abuse counselor. Through her I found out that there was an after school outpatient treatment program in the neighborhood for teens. It met twice a week. Most of the youth were court ordered to attend. The high-school didn't have the authority to order my youth to attend this program, but he didn't know that. I asked them to help me get him in, and I didn't let him know that not attending was an option. There he got some solid information about substance abuse and its consequences and learned some skills for avoiding peer pressure.

This program also did routine drug testing, with a policy of three dirty urine samples and you are out. He liked the counselors, enjoyed being in the group, and was able to stay clean for over two months before he failed his first test. It wasn't too many months after that when he got the third strike and was out. I was sorry he wasn't able to complete the program, but I think that this was a valuable experience in many ways. It was the first two months of sobriety he had had since grade school. He got to feel what it's like to face life without being high. He also attended his first AA meetings as part of the program, and got some much needed factual information. He witnessed other kids who had succeeded in completing the program and felt positive about their future.

It is easy to be discouraged when the young person you are trying to help persists in self-defeating behavior. Once you realize that you can only offer to assist them in finding help and accept that you have no control over the outcome, your life becomes simpler. You tell yourself that Rome wasn't built in a day and come to appreciate any lessons learned. The process of finding and using resources and evaluating their effectiveness provides a learning experience for the whole family.

The first year we had him with us we were dealing with a resistant, withdrawn teen. That was our Honeymoon period. The second year he started acting out more aggressively: getting into trouble at school, being truant, having to go to court, ignoring the judges' orders. His non-compliance brought him into the State's legal system. He was assigned a Probation Officer and now had access to social services funded by the County we lived in. Through his social worker I was able to push for him to be placed in a residential drug treatment program.

This program was in a ranch style house far from the city. The boys shared bedrooms and were under constant supervision. They attended classes right in the house. If they complied with the house rules during the week they could have a visitor on the weekend. Good behavior brought further privileges and I was able to take him to a movie matinee one weekend. He did well in this highly structured program. Eventually he earned the privilege of being off campus with me all day. I took him snowboarding for the first time. He looked like a different kid: excited, smiling, pink-cheeked flying down the hill. This was a happy day, but not the happy ending we all hope for. This type of treatment program is wonderful and effective. It is also very expensive and the stay too short.

Old habits die hard and once he was back in the city he fell back into the familiar groove of skipping school to get high with his friends.

I found a good male psychologist who diagnosed him for the first time with a severe attention deficit disorder. He put him on a non-addictive medication and I could see immediate improvement. I could only imagine how different his school experience would have been if someone had got onto this while he was still in grade school.

No parent wants to think there is anything wrong with their child. Intelligent children are often skilled at hiding serious learning disabilities. They pose as class clowns or outcasts, not understanding the nature of their difference. By now he was playing the role of the high school's handsome rogue. He had a girlfriend who seemed to enjoy being with a bad boy. This chapter of his life was about to close and a new one to begin.

My husband retired and we moved back home, taking our now 18 year old charge with us. We told him his lifestyle wasn't working for us and he'd have to find other accommodations. He found a place to live, and got a job. He had done some maturing, gained some self-confidence, and learned some communication skills in the two years he was with us. The man who employed him was able to see his strengths and was willing to mentor him, teaching him skills, holding him accountable, and promoting him after he'd proved himself to be dependable and hardworking. His old "friendships" from his druggie past fell away. The truth was he no longer fit in with his old friends. He had grown and changed. Now he sees those guys as a bunch of losers. He has made new friends at work who have encouraged him to stay clean, work out at a gym, and take care of his health. His self-esteem has risen considerably. He never finished high-school, but he passed the GED test easily. Today he is self-supporting and has stayed with the same employer for eight years learning new skills and earning several promotions. He comes over on Holidays. He gives us hugs. We wish him well.

My reason for writing about this very personal experience is to make the point that there is no magic bullet. We are all winging it. Sometimes it seems like you are not making any progress, but the little successes add up. The small gains accumulate, they are not lost. You can think of them as being in storage to be brought forward when the right circumstances occur.

When you feel discouraged and start thinking, "This kid will wind up in jail or on the streets," it's helpful to remind yourself of the fact that none of us knows the future. Maybe you've observed that the high-school star that everyone thought would be the greatest success isn't, and the guy who dropped out has invented something wonderful. Instead of projecting your worst fears onto your young person, use your concern to propel you to take positive action.

Over the years working with young people, I've come to believe the thing I've offered them of the greatest value is being respectful of them, even when they weren't exhibiting much self-respect. Equally important is modeling self-respect by maintaining reasonable but firm boundaries.

We have a built in impulse to protect our children from ever having anything bad happen to them. As adults we have witnessed tragedy. We want our youth to avoid the pitfall of substance abuse and the misery it brings. Sometimes parents are the last people teens want to listen to on this topic. If they've blocked our voice, we need to keep looking for one they will hear.

One good reason for seeking support for yourself in trying times, aside from protecting your own mental health, is that being able to talk through your own anxieties helps you get a broader perspective. You will see that just as others are able to help you, there will be people who will be there for your child in ways you can't predict.

I couldn't have imagined the level of support our youth got in his work environment. Miracles do happen!

Dealing with a teen with issues of drug abuse, delinquency or legal problems is difficult. The troubled youth being your biological child adds another layer of complexity. The mirror they present may reflect an aspect of yourself or your mate that you find upsetting. They may also remind us of times in our past we'd prefer to forget. They may evoke memories of our own parents or siblings that haunt us, making it hard to separate the past from the present when relating to them.

Sometimes parents' guilt over their own behavior and their desire to keep family problems secret stand in the way of getting help for their child. Staying mired in guilt can immobilize parents from being effective advocates for their child. The way to make amends for mistakes you've made in the past is to find people who can help your child now.

Help is always available to us in some form. Sometimes in order to accept it we have to first forgive ourselves for things we wish we had done differently. We may wonder about possible causes of our child's problems. Were we too strict, or too lenient? Was it our own past drug use? Was it because we got divorced? We can waste precious time mulling over the past and playing amateur psychologist. Time spent dwelling on the past is not only non-productive, but a distraction from taking action that can move the family in a more positive direction.

Another obstacle to finding the help needed to start the family on the path to recovery is the tendency to shift blame for the child's problems onto the other parent. This can become a deadly ping pong match.

Ping. "You weren't here when he needed you."

Pong. "You've spoiled him rotten."

Ping. "A fine example you've set for your son."

Pong. "You've babied him so much. He thinks he shouldn't have to do anything."

What is so seductive about these exchanges, which can go on for years without much change, is that they provide us with a way of projecting our guilt onto the other. This dynamic can continue as long as both parties continue to project guilt and blame onto each other rather than look inside, forgive, and move forward. Most people need outside help in recognizing and breaking destructive, repetitive behavior patterns. It can be done.

Working on easing the tensions in your primary relationship is an important first step in order to gain the strength and resolve needed to provide a united front. Working on team building and healthy boundaries will build confidence in your decision making process. This unity of purpose is necessary in order to move forward.

Rejecting blame as a way of punishing yourself or others will free creative energy. This will allow you to find solutions for the challenges that lay ahead. There is no "one size fits all" answer to these problems. Here are some of the questions you may have to find your own answers to:

- Do you feel that the substance abuse is at a level that inpatient treatment would be the best option? Can you afford it? Does your insurance cover it?

- Are you or your child eligible to receive social services?

- Is there Alanon or a parents' group in your area where you could find some emotional support and talk with people who may have already researched various programs and services in your community?

- Can you get help through your church or school?

Another possibility to consider, especially if your teen is involved with a peer group that is having a strong negative influence, is sending them to live temporarily with a relative in another city or state. If this seems to be your best option, it is important for the relative to understand what they are taking on and find out in advance what legal documents they might need to access services for the youth.

If your child is facing legal issues, does your community have a drug court that offers treatment for youthful offenders? If not, can you identify an appropriate treatment option to ask that the court consider? Sometimes getting a youth into treatment during the pretrial period can help. This is especially true if the youth co-operates with treatment and the center can give the judge a positive progress report.

A downside of teens getting involved in peer programs is the opportunity for kids who are looking for trouble to hook up with like-minded peers or to find youth more troubled than they are who may influence them to get involved in new negative behaviors. This risk is always a factor to consider. You have to ask yourself how naïve, suggestible, and easily led is your youth, and weigh this against the benefits the program offers. You can also bring this issue up with the staff before making a commitment.

Young people may experiment with substances that their parents might never consider them to be using or abusing. You may not smell alcohol on their breath and they may answer no when you ask them if they've been smoking pot, but your gut tells you that something is not right. Their eyes look glassy, dilated, vacant, or seem strange in some way. You are noticing changes in their behavior. They seem secretive, and you feel that you are not getting the straight story from them. You are uncomfortable with the people they are hanging out with, the hours they are keeping, etc. They may be sniffing solvents, glue or inhaling whatever substance is the current fad among their peers. They may be smoking "meth," or using a variety of prescription drugs illegally. Whether or not you know what they are using, it's important to seek help in dealing with the fact that you are uneasy with their behavior and concerned about what is causing the negative changes you are observing.

The difference between what they are telling you and what you are witnessing and feeling is troubling. You want to trust them. You don't want to believe that they aren't being honest with you, or that they are doing something harmful to their health behind your back. You don't want to seem paranoid, and you also don't want to ignore the fact that your radar is telling you that something is amiss. If you are having these feelings, it might be useful to keep a journal for a few weeks and write down the behaviors that you are observing that are making you uneasy. It might be useful to discuss them with a trusted family member. It may be the time to talk to the school counselor if your teen's grades are suffering. Don't hesitate to voice your concerns, and begin identifying helpful resources.

Sometimes parents ignore or minimize what is happening to their teen, because they are already under a lot of stress and don't want to identify yet another problem. Sometimes parents only want to see how smart, popular or beautiful their children are. It's hard in the midst of a busy life to keep your attention focused on those nagging concerns, and then take the action necessary to develop a well thought out plan for addressing them. We encourage you to do exactly that.

Educate yourself about what drugs are popular in your teen's environment. Synthetic drugs from China are being shipped to the U. S. in huge quantities. These chemicals are sprinkled onto shredded leaves, attractively packaged like trading cards and sold under various names like Vanilla Sky, Blueberry Haze, Florida Spice, etc. The labels say, "Not for human consumption." These dangerous drugs are being sold in local convenience stores, and kids are buying them on line. They think it's synthetic pot. According to research published in "JAMA Pediatrics," 11% of high school seniors engage in binge drinking, consuming ten or more drinks within a few hours, enough to lead to alcohol poisoning or even death.

Find out what's going on at their school, and with their peers. Most importantly, seek help as early as possible.

QUESTIONS

1. Do you know other parents who are having similar concerns, or could you find a way to identify and contact them?

2. Are you interested in forming a support group with them and sharing information on resources you find?

3. Could you see using some of the chapters of this book to help each other problem solve?

4. Are you interested in pushing for your local community to establish and provide drug treatment programs for youth?

CHAPTER 10. SPECIAL SITUATIONS AND ISSUES.

We have emphasized that each family must seek its own solutions to the problems that addiction creates for them. Simple or single solutions are generally inadequate to deal with the complex set of circumstances associated with addiction, and we have warned our readers to avoid people or groups that promise that they have the one answer.

We present a **method for finding individual solutions for families** that calls for development of seven specific skills that will help each family confront their individual situations successfully. That method and the skills on which it is based apply to the special situations and issues discussed in this chapter. The special circumstances discussed here elicit numerous questions from families and require special consideration.

A. Dual Diagnosis.

When a person is addicted to drugs or alcohol and also suffers from a mental illness, that person is considered to have a dual diagnosis.

Our intention throughout this book has been to avoid technical complexities or disputes that primarily concern professionals. We do not insist on the position, for example, that addiction is a disease; we simply note that the disease model of addiction gives the family a more effective way to understand what they are witnessing and take action to deal with the problems addiction presents.

In addition, we have avoided referencing the many useful books about addiction, preferring to simply talk to our readers from our own experience and professional expertise. In this chapter, we make an exception to this practice and recommend to families of dual diagnosis addicts that they read <u>At Wit's End: What You Need to Know When a Loved One is Diagnosed with Addiction and Mental Illness</u>, by Jeff Jay and Jerry A. Boriskin, PhD (Hazelden, 2007). This book provides an invaluable discussion of addiction and each of the co-occurring mental illnesses. While in our opinion it does not provide the detailed assistance that families need to deal with the practical aspects of coping with addiction, it does provide excellent background information.

In our experience, many families initially believe that if the addict in their family not only has a substance abuse problem, but has also been diagnosed as depressed, bi-polar, schizophrenic, or suffering from post-traumatic stress syndrome, their options for taking effective action are reduced or non-existent. While dual diagnosis does call for special consideration, the skills taught in this book can be highly effective both in improving the lives of family members of dual diagnosis addicts and in shaping the behavior of the addict in positive ways.

To focus our discussion, we'll use the example of a bi-polar addict. In addition to being a common combination of diagnoses, this example will clarify the relationship between the two and help explain how family solutions involve dealing with both more or less simultaneously.

Bi-polar disorder is characterized by alternating episodes of depression and manic thinking and acting. The typical bi-polar patient has mood swings that can operate in a more or less regular pattern, or can occur spontaneously and unexpectedly. During the manic phases, grandiose thinking and uncontrolled bursts of activity are common; judgment goes out the window, and any attempt by a family member or anyone else to reason with the bi-polar addict is usually seen as impertinent meddling by someone who just doesn't understand the grand designs of the addict. Anything the addict might have learned about managing his condition when not in the grip of mania seems to become irrelevant to the addict, and rash, dangerous adventures are likely.

Because the two poles of the disorder are almost opposites, it can be difficult to find a medication or combination of medications that is effective in moderating both the depression and the mania. In effect, medications that control the manic energy can worsen the depression, and medications that lighten depression can feed the mania.

For an addict who is struggling to build a life without his drug of choice, depression can have the effect of making the whole effort meaningless and unrewarding. The manic phase can make the effort of sobriety seem totally unnecessary and suitable only for lesser mortals.

Maintaining a balanced life, which is so important for continued sobriety, is the very antithesis of bipolar disorder.

This simplified description is used to present and discuss the challenges faced by individuals with this particular dual diagnosis and the difficulty family members have understanding and responding to the erratic moods and behaviors they observe.

We think it is important for families of dual diagnosis addicts to understand that their challenge is more complex, but not different in kind, from those dealing with addiction alone. The more out of touch with reality the addict is, the more firmly grounded the family must be. While it may take a family some period of time to understand the reality of dealing with a dual diagnosis addict, it will usually boil down to something like the following.

A dual diagnosis addict who is effectively medicated and who is under the care of competent mental health professionals can often function in a reasonably normal way as long as he is not actively using his drug of choice. Finding a good therapist who is willing to devise a comprehensive treatment plan and keep working on solutions to complex problems can be a challenge that requires commitment and persistence on the part of the family.

The anti-psychotic and anti-depressive medications usually prescribed are powerful, and they often have serious side-effects. Changes in the levels of these medications can have important effects as well, and generally any changes must be carefully considered and monitored by professionals. **These medications do not react well to the concurrent use of alcohol or non-prescription drugs.** As a result, irregular use of medications, or use of the addictive drug or alcohol along with these medications, can cause sudden and dramatic changes in behavior. The behavior of dual diagnosis addicts under these circumstances is generally well beyond the ability of most families to handle without the help of trained professionals.

Psychiatric wards, rehabilitation facilities, and detoxification centers are staffed with medical and other treatment professionals. They work in facilities that are designed to help them cope with erratic, violent, or unpredictable behavior. Obviously, families and homes are not so staffed and designed. Yet, it can take families a considerable period of time to realize that they are completely unsuited for dealing with an un-medicated or misdiagnosed mental patient, especially one who is abusing drugs or alcohol. Unless families understand this clearly and without guilt, they cannot effectively plan to deal with what they are facing.

The bottom line for families with dual diagnosis addicts is the same as for families facing any addiction: what are family members capable of handling and willing to deal with? And, can they develop a plan for dealing with situations that take them beyond that capability and/or willingness?

When the family understands and accepts their bottom line, they can communicate it to the addict verbally and through their actions. If the family itself is not clear about their bottom line, it's not reasonable to expect the addict, dual diagnosis or not, to understand or comply with it.

We suggest using the communication techniques discussed in Chapter 7 to convey to the addict that he needs professional care, and what your limitations are. It will be a relief to both of you to get real about the fact that you can't be your loved one's therapist and that your home is not a rehabilitation facility. You can offer assistance in locating appropriate services in your community or elsewhere if necessary. You can communicate your willingness to do whatever is necessary to keep yourself and the addict safe until he is able, with the help of professionals, to manage his condition at an acceptable level.

Dual diagnosis addicts, like other addicts, are responsible for managing their conditions. This is not a value judgment, but a simple statement of fact. If addicts are unwilling or unable to maintain their medication schedule or their sobriety, the family generally cannot manage those things for the addict, nor can they manage the behavioral consequences. Especially in the case of dual diagnosis, professional care and control are necessary.

If a dual diagnosis addict is acting in a dangerous, erratic, or threatening manner in public, the usual consequence is that someone notices, is concerned, and calls 911. The police are trained to determine whether the person should be confined, taken to the emergency room, or otherwise managed. Families must, in the last resort, be willing to call on the police to help get the addict under appropriate control and care until reasonable control can be achieved by the addict himself.

Dual Diagnosis and Insurance

In most cases, if you have a family member with a serious mental condition along with addiction, he is most likely eligible for Social Security Disability Insurance (SSDI) benefits. Detailed information about these benefits along with claim forms can be found in the Federal Government's Social Security Administration website.

The application process is cumbersome, and it is quite common to have your initial application denied. However, if your family member is truly disabled for work by a diagnosed mental illness, you can persist with your application, provide any additional medical documents or personal information needed, and succeed in establishing eligibility for the benefits. This can be important for several reasons.

Unless money is not an issue for your family, you may not be able to financially support even the basic needs of the addict. SSDI benefits include a monthly check that is often sufficient to cover most basic needs. More important, unless your family member already has good medical insurance, SSDI benefits include coverage under the Medicare program and under your State's Medicaid program. This is a huge benefit in securing space in treatment programs and even in hospital treatment. In addition, each state provides different levels and types of assistance to individuals covered under this umbrella program.

Having coverage under Social Security Disability Insurance can mean the difference between crushing financial burdens on the family along with non-availability of good treatment options on the one hand, and a wide network of financial and social support for your loved one on the other.

If no one in your family is capable of working through the bureaucratic system to secure SSDI benefits, some cities and states provide assistance with the process. As a last resort, there are private attorneys that can help you pursue a successful application.

B. Addiction and Violence.

Violence as defined here is not simply one event such as a physical confrontation, but a continuum of disrespect that often culminates in physical violence. This continuum may start with verbal aggression such as name calling, using a loud, aggressive voice tone, throwing objects, or damaging property in an effort to exert control over situations. You may find yourself walking on eggshells to keep the addict from getting angry, and doing things for the addict that they should be doing for themselves in an attempt to keep some level of peace in the family. Unfortunately this continuum of disrespect is always present at some level when someone is addicted to drugs or alcohol. Family members who are interacting with the addict in the family need to understand this continuum and know how to deal with it.

Experts look at the history of an individual to determine the likelihood that they will become violent in the future. If there is no prior history of violence, they presume that violent behavior in the future is unlikely. However, when you add addiction to the life of an individual who has no history of disrespect toward others or of physical violence, you are actually dealing with a different person with different capabilities than before they became addicted. Their past behavior pattern is no longer a safe predictor of future non-violence. You are now dealing with an individual who is no longer able to function in a normal manner because of changes to the brain as a result of addiction. The addiction is a new factor which may make aggressive behaviors more likely.

In addition, when the family begins to establish and enforce boundaries, the equilibrium the addict is used to begins to shift. One possible reaction by the addict is to add violence or the threat of violence to his repertoire of manipulation. The core team should be prepared for this.

You can prepare for the possibility of violence in two ways: work on prevention; and plan your response if violence does occur.

There is a theory in community law enforcement that small things lead to bigger things. If the community or its police force don't pay attention to the small problems or violations, people start to think that nobody cares and that they can get away with bigger things. This same dynamic applies to families. Becoming mindful of small things that go on in your family and how they might progress can save you grief in the future.

Everyone in the family must know that disrespectful behavior is not acceptable and will not be tolerated.

If the addict takes something they didn't ask for, or uses rough, harsh language toward a family member, they must get a clear message that this is not how people behave toward each other in the family. Do not let small escalations in aggression go unnoticed. If you tolerate or ignore the addict's aggressive verbal behavior, you may be unwittingly giving the message that this type of behavior is acceptable. That could lead to further aggression such as breaking things or punching holes in the walls.

If the addict in your family already has a history of violence, review how you've dealt with it in the past. What has worked and what hasn't?

The main focus of your actions and planning for the possibility of violence is to protect your own well-being. Your concern for the welfare of the addict must not overshadow the importance of putting your safety first. You can learn to act as your own advocate by seeking outside support. One of the advantages of having an outside support group is that other members have most likely dealt with this issue and can offer suggestions based on their experience. It helps to have somewhere to go where there are people you trust who will allow you to discuss the issues you are facing, and where you will be able to get honest feedback and advice.

Addicts have learned to not take responsibility for their behavior. This way of thinking is caused or reinforced by changes to the brain brought on by compulsive drug or alcohol use. Addicts are typically able to rationalize almost any behavior to control those close to them and shield themselves from the reality of their addiction. Addicts struggle to maintain the fantasy that they have everything under control and what they do is nobody's business.

Challenging this distorted view of the world can trigger aggressive behavior. With this in mind, if you plan to confront an addict with an unwelcome truth it may be wise to have a support person present. Honest and straight communication with the addict does not include disrespectful, aggressive or verbally abusive language by the family member delivering the message. Part of the core team work is learning to state what is true for you as calmly and non-judgmentally as possible.

Family members tend to build up a tolerance, not to drugs, but to crazier and crazier behavior until they are tolerating very unhealthy behavior in the addict, and accepting it as normal. Denial is sometimes as big a problem among family members as it is among addicts and can be just as destructive. The sooner you begin to see the reality of what is going on with the continuum of violence, the better chance you have for a healthier outcome for yourself and your family.

In order to intervene on the potential road to violence you need to start as early as possible to create and enforce boundaries with the addict. What is acceptable and what is not acceptable in your home? What are the consequences for unacceptable behavior?

Many families find it almost unthinkable that they would ever call the police for protection against a spouse or a son or daughter. This reluctance can mean that you allow the addict in your family to have a monopoly on violence in the service of his addiction. You must be able to involve the police if necessary, and the addict in the family must know that you are willing to do so. If you think you might need to call the police in the future to help enforce a boundary, don't wait until you need them to talk to them. Go to your local police station ahead of time. Let them know what you are dealing with and what you are trying to accomplish, so that if you do need their help they already know who you are.

Even if you are physically able to protect yourself against the addicted member of your family, as a general rule you should not take on the role of physically "handling" violence by the addict. Violence against members of the family or violence against your property should be dealt with as a law enforcement issue. Otherwise the addict may learn that it is acceptable to escalate the violence beyond what you are prepared to deal with.

It is extremely important not to isolate yourself with this problem. Reaching out for support in your community is essential, and is not an optional behavior if you are to have much of a chance of successfully dealing with family violence.

Be aware that if you are in a relationship with a person whose violent behavior predates the addiction, the addict is facing two separate issues. Treatment for the addiction can't be expected to resolve an established pattern of violent behavior. Anger management or other therapeutic interventions will most likely be necessary to address this tendency toward aggressive behavior. Generally, however, anger and control issues cannot be successfully treated until the addiction is under some degree of control.

Addiction does not just make a person more likely to engage in violence against others. It also makes it much more likely that the addict will himself be a victim of violence. Some types of addiction actually make the addict helpless against aggressive behavior and violence, and also undermine the addict's good judgment about putting himself in danger. A woman who is addicted is more likely to be vulnerable to sexual predators, sexual abuse and violence. A man who is addicted is more likely to be the victim of theft and assault.

Families tend to understand the greater vulnerability of their addicted members and to want to protect them against those dangers. This fear of what may happen to the addict is one of the most difficult obstacles to setting and maintaining boundaries. **The unfortunate truth which families must come to grips with is that a practicing addict cannot effectively be protected from the consequences of addiction.** As we discuss at length in other parts of this book, firm boundaries, **in the long run**, are the most effective way a family can practically influence the addict to seek real help. Protecting the addict from the natural consequences of his addiction is usually helpful only to prolong the addiction and enable the continuing enslavement to the addiction.

C. Formal Interventions.

Formal Interventions are structured meetings or confrontations between the family and the addicted family member. Generally the point of a formal intervention is to convince the addict to enter treatment immediately. A formal intervention is a highly choreographed method of giving straight, honest feedback to the addict about how their drug/alcohol use has affected each member of the family who participates in the meeting. The intervention may be guided by a trained professional who works with the family to create the structure that is presented at the intervention. There are potential benefits to formal interventions and there are some things to look out for.

Formal interventions are marketed by individuals and programs for profit. Sometimes the programs that provide intervention services can be overly aggressive with vulnerable families. They may promise extraordinary results and success rates that sound encouraging, or threaten dire outcomes if their services are not used. Success and failure are relative terms when it comes to recovery from addiction. Recovery from addiction is a long term process that may take years, whether or not an addict enters treatment at the time of the intervention.

It is very common for addicts to agree to go into treatment and then leave after a week or so. Many will actually complete treatment and relapse later. These possibilities are generally all part of the recovery process. It is possible for someone to enter treatment the first time, complete treatment and remain in recovery with no relapses for the rest of their life, but that is not the typical experience of addicts and families. If you are considering working with a professional and organizing a formal intervention, keep in mind that if your family member enters treatment the intervention company may see that as a success but it may be only the beginning of a long process for both you and the addict.

We are not opposed to formal interventions. However, **we want to emphasize the vital importance of developing a long term philosophy about addiction and the process of managing it, as opposed to placing all your hopes and expectations on a one-time event.**

Addiction has an effect on everyone in the family, and personal recovery from those effects is an issue for every member of the family. Addiction is a chronic illness that the addict must take responsibility for managing with the goal of remaining in recovery over a lifetime. Understanding this will help you develop boundaries and will also help you keep your perspective, whatever type of intervention process you engage in.

Without a long term philosophy you may get sucked into every twist and turn in the addict's drama. It is always good if an addicted person agrees to go into a treatment program. But treatment is not the endgame, nor does it ensure success. It is one step on a possible road to recovery.

D. Society and Addiction.

In Chapter 1 we said that people tend to view addiction as either a disease or a sign of flawed character. In terms of the larger society, these two views translate into seeing addiction as either a medical condition or as a legal issue.

The difference between perceiving addiction as a crime or as a public health issue is extremely important in understanding our confused response as a society. Our belief is that addiction is primarily a public health issue that sometimes leads people into criminal behavior. Just as family members are all affected by addiction in the family, so we as citizens are all affected by addiction in our community and in our nation.

Throughout history people have sought ways to alter their consciousness. Ancient cultures used plants and mixtures of naturally occurring chemicals. There were strict rules for using these "drugs," and they were generally used in a specific culturally appropriate ritual manner. Gradually, as these cultures have broken down under the pressure of modern life, the rules for using drugs disappeared. In addition, powerful new drugs have been manufactured which do not occur in nature. Legal prescription drugs like Vicodin and Oxycontin have taken on a second life as illegally trafficked drugs. Highly potent street drugs are manufactured and sold indiscriminately to adults and minors, often with sophisticated marketing and distribution systems.

Drug use has evolved into a personal ritual that is only governed by the individual person's ability or inability to control their use. In spite of many years of effort to regulate, control and punish the use of drugs, the United States is still the leading consumer of legal and illegal drugs in the world.

While significant efforts have been made to provide funds and facilities for treatment of drug abuse and addiction, our society has overwhelmingly chosen to consider drug use as a criminal matter. The amount of money devoted to prosecuting the criminal behavior that results from drug abuse and addiction dwarfs the resources devoted to treatment. Building prisons and incarcerating a higher percentage of our population than any other modern Western country, many on drug related charges, has clearly had a higher priority than providing treatment facilities and personnel.

Addiction is a chronic brain disease which has a serious effect on the addict's behavior. This leads to some drug users committing crimes, having serious medical problems that they would not have otherwise and a much higher incidence of incarceration, domestic violence, and child abuse and neglect than would normally exist in our society.

Families have learned that the key to progress in implementing behaviors that lead to a better life is a clear understanding of the nature of addiction. Our failure as a society to understand the nature of addiction is a major reason why addicts are not getting treatment, why treatment centers are not being funded, why families often struggle to find adequate resources to help addicted members and themselves, and why our jails are filled with people who are there because of their addiction.

There is a powerful segment of our society that helps drive the perception that drug use is highly desirable, exciting and meaningful. The alcohol, tobacco, pharmaceutical, and advertising industries spend billions of dollars to create compelling images of drug use as a life enhancing experience, sophisticated, romantic, or simply necessary. Tobacco is a perfect illustration of a substance that is legal for adults, highly addictive, and with absolutely no redeeming social value. In other words there is no way to use this substance that would not put the user at serious risk for addiction and for the host of diseases that tobacco use causes, starting with cancer and heart disease.

As a society we are confused about how we should respond to addiction. All people tend to agree with the basic fact that addiction is not good. But what do we do about it? How do we respond? That is where we get confused. The research shows that drug addiction is a brain disease and must be treated as a medical condition. Drug addicts often commit crimes in support of their addiction. Treatment must be the primary response, whether the addict is incarcerated or not. The recidivism rate for incarcerated addicts is clear evidence that prison without treatment does not inhibit drug-related criminal activity.

Where does this leave families? Because of the confused response we have as a society, families are conflicted about how to respond to addiction.

Because of our society's failure to send clear messages that addiction is a disease process that can happen to anyone, family members feel ashamed and isolated, and this results in a fear of seeking help.

There is a general perception that people are helpless in the face of addiction in the family when they are not. Our goal in this book has been to help clear up some of the misunderstandings about addiction and help family members understand what they are dealing with and how to deal with it. Following the concepts in this book will assist families to develop a response that will cut through the conflicting messages about drugs that have saddled our society with an unwinnable "war" on drugs.

As a society we have made some inroads against the use of alcohol and tobacco. Families who have borne the brunt of society's inability to effectively deal with these legal drugs have fought back with promising results. "Mothers Against Drunk Drivers" has successfully lobbied for both legislation and societal consciousness raising to reduce the carnage related to drinking and driving. Lawsuits against tobacco companies have exposed some incredible scandals related to false advertising and criminal adulteration of legal substances to make them more addictive. Still, these legal drugs remain an extensive public health problem comparable to the problems related to illegal drug use.

CHAPTER 11. HEALING YOUR OWN LIFE.

There is a temptation for family members to think they must be instrumental in creating a cure for the addict. Loving caregivers often feel that if they try hard enough they will be successful, and that somewhere there is a magic key that when found and used effectively will overcome an addict's pursuit of their drug and stop them on their self-destructive path.

Many addicts do find their way into recovery, but in reality many remain addicted regardless of any and all efforts of their caregivers. Failing to address this reality would be a disservice to families.

Hopefully, this book has helped you to have a better understanding of your limitations in creating outcomes for the addict. What we want to address in this chapter are some things you can do to create better outcomes for the person you have the most control over—yourself.

Any step you take toward taking better care of yourself physically and emotionally will help you gain a clearer perspective on what your priorities need to be. By taking concrete action to improve your own wellbeing you are affirming that life is valuable, and that you deserve to live it to the fullest. Years of being emotionally attached to an addict creates an incredible drain on your energy. It distorts your perspective on what your life is and can be. Those of us who felt that being happy again wasn't a possibility have been surprised to find that life can indeed be good again, whether the addict is using or not.

It is common for people to put so much of their time and energy into helping their loved one that their own life begins to shrink and some aspects of it may disappear altogether—friendships fall by the wayside, medical appointments are missed, vacations don't happen, etc. Family members may lose sight of their own needs and interests. Changing patterns of self-neglect may feel unnatural, as though you are being irresponsible or abandoning the addicted family member. We want to assure you that this is not the case. Remember, our forefathers thought the pursuit of happiness was so important that they included it in the Declaration of Independence. We want to help you make your own declaration and find your way back to a happier, more fulfilling life.

If you decide that you do want to take better care of yourself, and you are approaching this challenge as part of a family team, one of your best resources can be family members' memories of things you used to do for fun. Was it hiking, thrift store hunting, playing card games, skating, or bowling?

One week in Bob's family group he asked the women present to practice shifting their focus from the addict to themselves by doing something during the following week that would just be for their own pleasure. When they walked into group the following week they all had new hairdos. Without any discussion among themselves they had all picked getting their hair done. This was an activity they all remembered as being pleasurable and stress reducing. When they returned to group they had the added bonus of telling each other how great they looked and laughing about how each of them had come up with the same idea.

The rest of this chapter gives some examples of activities the authors have found personally rewarding or have seen friends or support group members use to open their lives to enjoyment or pleasure. There is one general rule to remember when doing these activities with friends or family: **avoid talking about the addict and problems associated with addiction.** If the activities you choose are solitary, **don't allow yourself to ruminate about addiction issues. Do something that allows you to be completely absorbed in the activity itself.**

Mental activities that demands your attention-- Sudoku puzzles, chess games, duplicate bridge games, crossword puzzles, scrapbooking, drawing, painting, journaling, reading, computer time—all these can be great distractions from worry.

Taking a short car trip to a cider mill or pumpkin patch in the Fall, walking in the park, listening to music you love, star gazing: these simple activities can lift your spirits.

It helps to find friends who are willing to do an activity with you; swimming, roller skating, dancing, hiking, or listening to live music together. If you enjoy reading, book clubs can be a way to meet others who share your interests.

One of the best ways to reduce stress is regular physical exercise.

- Walking, whether alone or with a family member or friend, is one of the best activities for improving both physical and mental health. Start slowly and increase your time by a couple of minutes every two weeks. Treat yourself to a good pair of walking shoes. Find a walking buddy if you can, and vary your route to keep up your interest. Wearing a pedometer can make it more fun. Don't forget to warm up and cool down. A friend who lives in a cold climate created a group of "mall walkers" so they wouldn't have to cancel their walks in winter weather. You can find information on local walking and hiking groups on-line.

- Many communities have a variety of exercise classes: Zumba, Pilates, Aerobics, etc. Yoga and Tai Chi combine physical activity with relaxation techniques. Local YMCA's offer a variety of classes along with exercise equipment and instruction. Some hospitals offer wellness programs that include exercise. All of these activities get you out into the community, meeting new people, and building your physical and emotional resilience.

- Gardening, whether growing vegetables to eat, or ornamental plants and flowers is relaxing. It is something you can do on a small or large scale. Growing a variety of violets under lights in an apartment can be just as rewarding as having a large outdoor garden. The idea is to be able to lose yourself in a pleasurable activity that absorbs your whole attention.

- If you used to play a musical instrument, painted, or worked with clay, this can be a good time to rekindle your creativity. Community colleges are good resources for adults looking to brush up old skills or learn new ones.

- In our community a dedicated group of women get together once a week to knit and "talk story." For many years they have made beautiful, hand-knit caps and booties for all the new babies born in our local Children's Hospital. These women have formed a strong social support for themselves in the process of doing charitable work.

Introduction to Meditation.

We end this chapter with a detailed discussion of meditation because it is an ideal counter to the stress of dealing with addiction.

Meditation encourages mindfulness in the present. The natural tendency of many people who are dealing with addiction is to focus on past disappointments and anxiously anticipate future problems. The more our fears have been validated in the past, the more likely we are to suffer from fear or worry about what might happen next. Meditation is one way to reduce the tendency to replay dreadful past experiences or project future problems that may or may not materialize. It brings our awareness to the present and what is appropriate for right now.

Meditation is an excellent way to begin to take control of your environment. That's because your "inner" environment is the most important part of your world, and has the most to do with how you, personally, experience everything, including how you respond to the challenges addiction presents. It is a place to find moments of complete peace.

Meditation is non-denominational. You don't have to belong to any particular religion or espouse any one religious belief to practice meditation. Every religion includes some type of devotional or meditational practice, and meditation doesn't conflict with any religious affiliation.

Many people think it isn't possible for them to meditate because their mind is too busy. This section will give you simple instructions to help you give it a try. If you find meditation useful, your practice may expand to the point where it's not just a coping mechanism, but an approach to life that gradually affects your attitudes and has positive effects on all of your relationships.

To begin meditating:
- Sit comfortably in a place and at a time when you're not likely to be disturbed.
- Sit with your back straight. Everything else about how you sit is optional. You can use a

chair, sit on a cushion, sit on the floor with your legs crossed, or however you are most comfortable. If you sit on the floor, you'll find it's important to sit on something high and firm enough that your knees are lower than your torso.
- Breathe.
- Give attention to your breath.
- Follow your breath, and pay attention only to your breath going in and out.
- Continue this breathing with focused attention for two or three minutes.

You have begun to meditate. You are being mindful of something: your breathing. You are not being mindful of anything else.

Notice what happened when you followed the directions above for a couple of minutes. Were you able to keep your full attention on your breath for more than a couple of breaths? It is a very common experience for your mind to lose track of your breath and wander off on random topics: what you need to do today, a conversation you had with your mother yesterday, where and what you plan to eat for dinner. That's just what the mind does. It likes to stay busy. It likes to jump around. You haven't failed. All that's necessary is to notice the mind drifting, and then return your focus, your mindfulness, to your breath.

When you do this exercise for the first time, a couple of things may happen. You might be surprised at how hard it is to keep the mind focused on what is going on in the present, and how much the mind wants to be somewhere else: in the past, in the future, anywhere but the present moment, where you're just sitting here watching your breath.

The second common experience is an unexpected sense of relief or relaxation, maybe even nostalgia. Turning your attention away from the automatic "thinking" the mind does when unattended can be deeply restful and peaceful.

A natural, normal result of spending a few moments at rest in awareness is centeredness and peace. The breath is a means and a method of recalling your attention to the present, a way for you to witness your present state of being.

If you allow yourself that experience, and are able to return to it on a regular basis, even for very short periods of time, you will experience significant positive changes. There are many things going on in all our lives that work against this natural tendency toward peaceful and restful meditation. We are used to feeding our overactive minds with planning, worrying, controlling, and obsessing on topics that keep us distressed.

That's why those of us who are interested in discovering and returning to that quiet place may need some special assistance to get there.

Here are a few ways to develop habits that encourage and assist us in spending more time in that peaceful place.

- Set aside a time or times during the day for focused awareness. Some people like to meditate in the morning before their regular day's activities begin. Some like to have time in the evening or later at night. Regularity is the key.

- Use the same quiet place every day for your quiet time. Try to find a place that's easy, convenient, and comfortable, where you aren't likely to be disturbed.
- Start by trying to meditate for a short period. Five minutes or so is adequate at the beginning. When you find yourself able to sit for longer, go ahead and extend it little by little, up to about twenty minutes at a time for the first several months.
- Set a minimum time that you want to stay in one position. You need not be a clock watcher, but do set the time.
- Remember there is nothing you're trying to achieve, no state of being you're trying to get to. Just pay attention to the breath. When your attention wanders, keep recalling your attention, your mindfulness, to your breathing process.

When you meditate, you are storing up a special kind of personal energy, which you can then apply to any area of your life.

There are lots of ways to get started meditating. If the way we've described here is too solitary for you, there are many alternatives. All metropolitan areas have meditation centers that include a variety of approaches to meditation. The one that we've described above is called Insight Meditation. If you're interested in finding a teacher or group, do a little research on the web and see what's available in your area.

If you choose to begin meditating on your own, we recommend that you read: <u>Mindfulness in Plain English</u>, by Bhante Henepola Gunaratana. One advantage of beginning with this book is that the same author wrote a second book in the same user-friendly style that's a great sequel: <u>Eight Mindful Steps to Happiness</u>. There are many other books on meditation, but these two are excellent introductory books for beginners.

Conclusion.

"Healing Your Own Life" is the last chapter in this book, but it could just as well be the first. At some point families of addicts come to the realization that they have to start taking care of themselves or they will be worse off than the addict they have been trying to help.

The 'Families and Addiction' blog has been on the Internet since 2006. During that time people from all over the world have accessed it, and the topics of most interest to them are those universal addict behaviors of denial, dishonesty, and manipulation. In a relationship with an addict, the only way to counter these negative patterns is to learn the skills necessary to shift the focus from the addict to taking care of yourself.

This book is about the process of learning to respond to addiction on your own terms. The biggest obstacles to overcome are isolation, shame, fear, anger, and trying to control things you have no control over.

We have emphasized the importance of getting and using an effective support system. We believe it's possible in most communities to find or create a supportive, non-judgmental group of people who are struggling with the same issues. If your group doesn't include a leader with solid knowledge and experience with addiction, we hope you will find this book a reliable and sympathetic guide.

There are big challenges in dealing with addiction in the family and big rewards as well. What may at first appear to be a hopeless situation can be an opportunity to find the peace and freedom you might have thought impossible. Those of us who have loved an addict feel marked by what we have been through. We will never be the same; carefree innocence is gone forever. What we have gained is a deeper understanding of ourselves and an appreciation for our own ability to survive and prosper through adversity.

ACKNOWLEDGMENTS

We are grateful to friends and family members, most notably Sue Brown and Francie Nolan, who made substantive contributions during the editing process. Michael Nolan and Carl Gallagher read early drafts of this book and encouraged us throughout the process. We appreciate all their support.

Our special thanks to Holli Corbett for her patience and professionalism in designing the book cover.

Printed in Great Britain
by Amazon